D1356457

KU DON

FASHION
BEYOND
VERSAILLES

FASHION BEYOND VERSAILLES

CONSUMPTION AND DESIGN IN SEVENTEENTH-CENTURY FRANCE

DONNA J. BOHANAN

LOUISIANA STATE UNIVERSITY PRESS
BATON ROUGE

Published by Louisiana State University Press
Copyright © 2012 by Louisiana State University Press
All rights reserved
Manufactured in the United States of America
First printing

Designer: Barbara Neely Bourgoyne
Typefaces: Arno Pro, Text; Engravers MT and Din Schrift, display
Printer: McNaughton & Gunn, Inc.
Binder: Acme Bookbinding, Inc.

Library of Congress Cataloging-in-Publication Data
Bohanan, Donna, 1954–
  Fashion beyond Versailles : consumption and design in seventeenth-century France /
Donna Bohanan.
    p. cm.
  Includes bibliographical references and index.
  ISBN 978-0-8071-4521-0 (cloth : alk. paper) — ISBN 978-0-8071-4522-7 (pdf) — ISBN
978-0-8071-4523-4 (epub) — ISBN 978-0-8071-4524-1 (mobi) 1. Fashion—France—
History—17th century. 2. Nobility—France—Social life and customs—17th
century. 3. Elite (Social sciences)—France—History—17th century. 4. Consumption
(Economics)—France—History—17th century. I. Title.
  TT504.6.F7B64 2012
  746.9'2—dc23
                                                                                    2011043188

The paper in this book meets the guidelines for permanence and durability
of the Committee on Production Guidelines for Book Longevity of the
Council on Library Resources.
∞

For Cynthia Ackermann-Bohanan

and

in memory of

Belinda Bohanan

CONTENTS

ACKNOWLEDGMENTS

This book started years ago in the archives of Grenoble, while I was there to work on a different project. I was examining a series of seventeenth-century household inventories in order to gain a sense of the wealth of noble families. These sorts of inventories, prepared by notaries at the death of a testator, have become the stock of material culture studies. I was soon captivated by the contents of these families' residences; I felt as if I were the ultimate interloper, and I relished it! In reading the detailed lists and descriptions of the objects that filled noble homes, I wondered more and more about how families actually lived with their possessions, how these objects shaped their daily lives, and how they used them to define themselves. And so this book began in the archives and with the inventories; only later did I set out in search of the literature to help me understand my documents. I am indebted to the staffs of the Archives Départementales de l'Isère and the Bibliothèque Municipale de Grenoble.

Back in the United States, the production of this project benefited enormously from the support of Auburn University, in particular the History Department. My department chairs, Bill Trimble, Tony Carey, and Charles Israel, arranged my schedule to give me time in the archives and allow for blocks of time in which to write. My cherished colleagues, Daniel Szechi and Ralph Kingston, listened cheerfully and never failed to offer invaluable suggestions. Christopher Ferguson was a gold mine of bibliographic suggestions, especially pertaining to early modern Britain. Joseph Kicklighter was, as always, my stalwart mentor and friend.

I also want to thank my acquisitions editor at LSU Press, Alisa Plant. I first met her at a meeting of the Southern Historical Association in Birmingham, Alabama. She was quick to express real interest in the project and never gave up on it or me, this despite my innumerable delays and pleadings for extra time. Teresa Rodriguez cheerfully worked with little notice to produce her inspired interpretations of period furnishings. They are wonderful. And I am indebted to my copy editor, Grace Carino, who painstakingly corrected and edited my manuscript.

Finally, much gratitude goes to those who were there day in and day out, my family. My parents, Donald and Jean Bohanan, have always supported me in every way they can, not the least of which is reminding me of my deadlines and my tragic tendency to procrastinate! My sister and brother-in-law, Cindy and Paul Ackermann, took me into their Swiss home weekend after weekend and sent me renewed and reenergized on Sunday evenings back to the archives in Grenoble.

I owe no greater debt than to Frank Smith, my husband, who held down the fort and took care of Sutyi, Axel, and Nola while I was absent from home for long periods. As always, he proofread and edited this manuscript in his incisive and dramatic manner.

Finally, my sisters, Cindy and Lindy, inspired this project. From Arkansas to Switzerland, in *brocantes,* flea markets, and antique shows, they revealed to me the thrill of the hunt. This book is for them.

FASHION
BEYOND
VERSAILLES

INTRODUCTION

This is a book about things. By things, I mean the possessions that accumulate during a lifetime and, at death, are inventoried and dispersed to heirs. In a sense it is a book about material culture, but it is not about the actual things themselves. This is not a study of the objects; it is not a history of the decorative arts. It is social history, a book about what things can tell us about the lives and lifestyles of their owners. The larger issue is how people used their goods, why they purchased them, and what goods meant in their social worlds. I base my remarks on notarial descriptions of objects, which offer a particular observation point.

What we now know about the late seventeenth and eighteenth centuries is that the demand for necessities and fashionable luxuries grew by revolutionary proportions, thereby providing a very important stimulus for economic growth and industrialization. McKendrick, Brewer, and Plumb were among the first historians of the eighteenth century to offer ample evidence for the important role of consumption in economic development, in their case British development.[1] Historians of eighteenth-century France, such as Daniel Roche, Annik Pardailhé-Galabrun, Colin Jones, and Rebecca Spang, have also described the rise of the consumer and, in the process, have challenged the older view that painted France as an underdeveloped nation of dispirited peasants and parasitic aristocrats. Recent historians have argued for a more vigorous economy in the eighteenth century, and among the evidence they cite is a new consumerism, a trend that extended well back into the preceding century.[2] The households I consider were inventoried during the late seventeenth and early eighteenth centuries, roughly the period 1680 to 1715, the point at which the consumption of nonessential goods began to take off in France. These developments were the antecedents to the rise of modern consumerism.

I will argue that such rising levels of consumption had special social significance in Dauphiné, a locale that had earlier endured a fiercely contested struggle over efforts to make nobles pay the detested tax known as the taille. As part of the debate over traditional tax exemptions for the nobility, the opposition mounted a rhetorical campaign challenging the nobles' rights and questioning their antiquity and integrity. Royal government, by its financial policies and judicial responses to the local cases at the heart of the crisis, served as a catalyst for social conflict in the region. In the end, the conflict known as the *procès des tailles* was resolved in a manner that emphasized more than ever the antiquity of a family and its concurrent lifestyle. By 1680, the *procès des tailles* was forty years past, and I invoke its lingering memory as meaningful political context for elite patterns of consumption.

The first chapter of this book focuses on the sociopolitical world of these consumers and establishes the importance of consumption and display. To contextualize elite consumption, it considers the crisis of regional politics and changing ideas of nobility—this in addition to cultural forces, such as the ideology of taste, that shaped nobles' consumer choices. The remaining chapters are each constructed around a particular type of goods or furnishings. In discussing these, I examine their impact on the life of the owner, the potential reasons for their purchase, and what ownership and exhibition tell us about changes in aristocratic society.

Chapter 2 deals with nobles' acquisition of objects that communicated ideas of magnificence and connoisseurship in a direct, unambiguous, and traditional manner. These included paintings, tapestries, Oriental rugs, and clocks, among other things, the traditional luxury goods to which only wealth gave access, and their display made a clear and dramatic statement about the taste of the owner. As time passed, the standard of magnificence moved beyond the acquisition of specific goods to incorporate various theories of style. Chapter 3 considers the principles that guided French style as it matured and the methods employed to create a unified, harmonious effect. To achieve that kind of harmony and unity, known as *regularité*, the French made extensive use of a single color or color scheme or single textile. The use of matched sets of furnishings, or seriality, often enhanced this unified effect. The growing use of more comfortable furniture, considered in Chapter 4, illustrates the evolution of the idea of luxury, an unfolding that involved not the abandonment of the exotic and opulent but a broadening cultural notion of luxury that embraced much of what, judged by modern standards, would appear rather practical. Comfort came forth as a new form of luxury that defined the relationship between sumptuousness and necessity.

Finally, Chapter 5 is about dining and entertaining. In serving their guests a new style of cuisine, noble families conveyed a new appreciation of food and good taste. Approaches to cooking changed, and so did the role of host and hostess; medieval forms of hospitality gave way to the rise of more modern and intimate forms of sociability. Furnishings for entertaining and for tablescapes proliferated during the period as recipes became more numerous and the basic design of menus more elaborate. To navigate *à table* required awareness of a prescriptive literature on etiquette and civility that addressed the details of dining, the use of utensils, and other recondite aspects of comportment at meals. These demands only reflected the changes in elite society that accompanied its adoption of the new cuisine.

Several important underlying assumptions about elites and consumption have shaped my approach to these topics. When I consider what noble families bought to furnish and decorate their households, I borrow from the social construct of class. In this regard, I am influenced by the work of David Parker, who advances a class-based analysis of French society.[3] Much about aristocrats' lifestyle depended on money, and we clearly see the power of money in their selection of household goods. Does this make French society a class-based one? No, but it does suggest that one can on occasion see the faint contours of class. Yet I believe that France continued to function still as a society of orders in which nobles enjoyed honor and esteem as a result of their function. Money was important to esteem and honor as well. It seems reasonable to believe that both class and order could have existed simultaneously. In this, I am influenced by the work of James Collins, who argues precisely so.[4] He maintains that seventeenth-century Breton society functioned within two hierarchical systems, either order or class, depending on the issue. In Dauphiné, the battle over the taille revealed the classlike characteristics of provincial society.

By focusing on Dauphiné, this study moves beyond Paris and Versailles and considers consumption patterns at the periphery of the realm. Much has been written about consumption in Paris (especially during the eighteenth century), significantly less about provincial consumption.[5] The consumption habits and decorative tastes of elites living at the periphery all point to the pull of the fashion gravity of the center and a closer integration of markets. News of Parisian fashions spread, more quickly than in times past, to the provinces, where elites were keenly interested in purchasing similar items. Does this mean that nobles' homes in Grenoble were all brilliantly appointed and mirrored the *hôtels* of Paris? Of course not. What it means is that provincial consumers bought the luxury goods of Paris and mimicked the fashions of Paris to the extent that money and access permitted them. What families created in Grenoble were homes that effected Parisian style in a diluted manner by the purchase of certain emblematic elements. That we know the same elements occurred in the homes of nobles in the Bordeaux region supports the assumption of a closer consumer and cultural relationship between center and periphery nationally.

Foreign responses to French—that is, Parisian—style, positive and negative, not only denoted a growing awareness of France as trendsetter but also set the standardization for elite material culture. That English aristocrats sought French or French-trained chefs for their kitchens is indicative of a degree of homogenization and internationalization of elite culture. From the reign of Louis XIV on, French tastes defined crucial aspects of that culture; more and more elites looked to Paris as fashion central. By their decorative choices, Dauphinois elites joined the growing international, even transatlantic, world of those on top.

This integration of the French and international luxury markets was driven by the truly herculean force of fashion. The works of Daniel Roche have particularly informed this book, and I believe that style and the desire to own the latest styles created a powerful desire to shop. The twin ideas of novelty and obsolescence, the mainsprings of fashion, were powerful motive forces in the late seventeenth century, as they are now.[6] Socially, fashion exerted boundless influence and energy, particularly when it partnered with that other great consumer force—emulation. The desire to achieve distinction through mimicry, by imitating the lifestyle and appearance of one's social superiors, seductively drove many families into the marketplace. But as important a force as emulation was to the seventeenth century, even more fundamental was mere fashion.

Fashion, or *la mode,* historically has been associated with women. Western civilization, in recent times, has classified shopping as women's work and has passed judgment on it. There is no doubt that fashion and consumption are subjects that raise important and persistent questions about gender; nor to my mind is there any doubt that men valued fashion and shopping much as women did. I do not consider gender in this study, except for brief reflection on the close association of fashion and women, because my sources do not allow for its consideration. A few of the inventories were the estates of women, and their contents did not vary from those of men; it is impossible to know who, husbands or wives, purchased those goods. I operate on the assumption, perhaps flawed, that both sexes played a determining role in the acquisition of many of the family's possessions, their cooperative goal being the construction of elite identity.

To understand that identity, and the crucial components thereof, I rely on postmortem household inventories. Upon the death of a family member, prior to the execution of his or her will, heirs enlisted the services of a notary to conduct an inventory of the deceased's household. These inventories are singular historical sources that allow modern scholars to mentally poke around and rifle through the contents of a household. There simply is no other type of historical document that yields as much information about household possessions.

What do we know about the inventory? First, we know it was legally mandated that it had to take place no earlier than three days—and no later than three months—after the death. These directives were certainly honored more in the breach than in the observance. Inventories were nowise universal. Families requested that a notary catalog the contents of a household when the heirs were minors requiring a guardianship; when the heirs simply wanted one to be done; and when the surviving spouse requested that the property in the estate be divided among children in anticipation of remarriage. Estimates indicated that few deaths actually resulted in estate inventories.[7]

The inventory, while a gold mine of information, is highly problematic as a historical document. Annik Pardailhé-Galabrun, whose beautifully detailed study of Parisian households in the eighteenth century, *The Birth of Intimacy*, is based on inventories, has written with great authority on the limitations of the postmortem inventory. She points out that the inventory does not provide much of an idea about the external appearance of the house or its internal layout. It is impossible to envision a blueprint because the notary never mentioned how he entered a room, from which direction, nor did he mention any passageways or staircases. Similarly, servants' quarters are ignored because they contained the servant's personal possessions.[8] Occasionally a Dauphinois notary referred to a bed that was reserved for a servant's use, but that constituted the full extent of such references.

Additionally, it is important to remember that in many instances the inventory likely was not comprehensive. No doubt heirs, spurred by greed and sibling rivalries, surreptitiously removed some items. The contents of homes were frequently edited, indeed looted, by heirs anxious to secure their claimed rightful share or to lay hands on that which they particularly coveted. And, in the end, the inventory is merely a list of goods named and described by the notary. We view the contents of a home through his filter. As Pardailhé-Galabrun notes, detail and accuracy depended on the "cultural sophistication of the notary."[9]

I do not offer these inventories as a statistical sample, nor is this a quantitative study. The number of extant inventories is small but sufficiently meaningful for many purposes. I was first attracted to these inventories because of an interest in local politics and later realized their contents showed consumption to be an urgent issue for these families. I found that by putting inventories to a different kind of scrutiny, they yielded different sorts of information. This book is therefore unlike studies that have used quantification to produce important findings about the appearance of and desire for nonessential goods. Precisely because the number of inventories is limited, it affords the opportunity to look beyond single items and to consider the relationship of one item to another, one residence to another.[10] My goal has been to move beyond the history of disembodied things and consider the object in a larger context, to look at the society of the object. I am interested in objects as social artifacts, that is, what they can tell us about social values and ways of living.

LE PAYS

NOBLES, TASTE, FASHION, AND POLITICS

In the late sixteenth and early seventeenth centuries, the nobility of Dauphiné, a province located at the periphery of the realm, and one traditionally sheltered from the grasping fiscal reach of central government, became deeply embroiled in a great conflict over taxation and aristocratic privilege. Dauphiné was a *pays d'états,* a semiautonomous province where the issues of provincial rights and privileges defined much of its institutional and political history. Here the crown's efforts to increase taxation ignited the *procès des tailles,* a prolonged contest between the nobility and the crown on one the hand and the nobility and the Third Estate on the other: a struggle that revealed deep divisions between the estates. In protecting its interests, the Third Estate challenged traditional aristocratic privileges to such an extent that the fundamental rationale for the existence of nobility came under attack. As it developed, the conflict in Dauphiné brought into focus the growing horizontal and classlike divisions in provincial society.[1]

CHANGES IN THE NOBILITY

At the same time that the Dauphinois nobility came under assault by the Third Estate, nobles throughout France were experiencing a kind of cultural and social metamorphosis that ultimately changed the very meaning of the term *nobility*. This change provided a vital social and cultural context for the great provincial conflict over taxation. As part of this prolonged and divisive episode, the local nobility's acquisition of goods assumed greater meaning—an attempt at self-reconstruction as a response, perhaps an un-conscious one, to class conflict and the policies of central government.

The late sixteenth century, a time at which the tax controversy reached fevered pitch, was an overall period of crisis and criticism for the tradi-tional nobility of France. Numerical decline (at least temporarily), eco-nomic hardship, dilution by intermarriage with the bourgeoisie, erosion of political power, and the emergence of criticism that questioned the real need for the existence of the nobility combined to bring about a profound transformation within the noble ranks.[2] No challenge faced was more threatening to the nobility's raison d'être than the Military Revolution.

From the time of the Hundred Years' War the advantages provided by gunpowder and contemporary infantry tactics as decisive factors in war had been clear. Time had supplanted the dominant mounted warrior noble with the firearmed common foot soldier. With this change the military rationale for a fighting nobility—and, by extension, its claim to a privileged place in European society—came to an end. The new reality of warfare, exacer-bated by frequently unacceptable conduct and excesses during the Wars of Religion, focused social attention to question the traditionally professed ideal of nobility in the late sixteenth century. Nobility, its defenders argued, was virtue, demonstrated by one's exemplary conduct. Yet old noble families had run amok during the wars, belying this ideal with behavior far from vir-tuous. They had disgraced themselves and in the process were revealed ig-noble and no better than anyone else. These events and attitudes accelerated changes, as the events of the Wars of Religion provoked a great moral debate about the fundamental concepts of nobility. Critics wrote of nobles' igno-rance and anti-intellectualism, and their perceived backwardness was the subject of numerous pamphlets and treatises. At this time many lost political power and offices to better-educated members of the middle class, and apol-ogists offered a program for rehabilitation of the nobility, proposing educa-tional reform as the primary means to restore its virtue and to retain power.[3]

One important outcome of this discourse was the emergence of a rede-fined idea of nobility that better accommodated social reality. Ellery Schalk has described how attitudes toward the nobility changed substantially during the sixteenth and seventeenth centuries, how perceptions of nobles evolved from the medieval warrior to the modern aristocrat—educated, sophisticated, and cultivated.[4] By the end of the sixteenth century a new paradigm of virtue also emerged, no longer redolent solely of the warrior image but defined more inclusively, in a way that justified a place for the robe families, the newly ennobled families within the privileged rank.

The Wars of Religion had engendered new antagonisms between elites and the common people, and elites closed ranks in a common defense based on race to maintain a naturally and hierarchically ordered society. Both the old and more recently ennobled families relied on assertion of their natural superiority to retain their privileged status and to defend themselves from the disorder threatened by those beneath them.[5] These changes reflected the basic social reality that birth had replaced valor as the basis of nobility. Other broad social and cultural forces also propelled this evolution.

Historians have argued that elite society self-consciously refashioned itself in an effort to maintain separation and distinction from popular culture. In other words, elites purposefully pulled away and distanced themselves from popular culture in a variety of ways. Differences in literacy and formal education played an obvious role in this process, but there were other, more subtle social dichotomies as well. Refinement of manners, or comportment, was another method by which elites sought to achieve distance from the lower orders. They created this distinction with complex codes of etiquette and civility. The significance given to proper etiquette underscored the fact that early modern Europe remained to a considerable extent a society of orders in which aristocratic identity and prestige rested on honor and esteem, that is, on social opinion. One's behavior and the response it evoked were definitive and together constituted the accepted social norm that viewed nobles as honorable and worthy of the privileges conferred on them.[6] Etiquette became a major force in the society and culture of French nobles because its observance allowed them to reinforce ideas of distinction and honor. With the court as the model, civility evolved as an elaborately codified means to display publicly the rank or status of an individual.[7]

Early modern thought embraced the concept of *honnêteté,* a term that incorporated a moralistic quality into the definition of civility. *Honnêteté* referred to refinement and virtue, and it apparently developed in opposition to certain court society behavior that some criticized for its excesses. For the critics, *honnêteté* reflected restraint and the idea of *proper* behavior.[8] In the *honnête homme,* or honest man, one finds more than mere charm and grace: the *honnête homme* exhibited a defining moral and intellectual quality.[9] By the early seventeenth century, nobles had access to a large and growing literature beginning with the prototype, Castiglione's *Courtier,* and including, among other titles, Nicolas Faret's widely read *The Honnête Homme, or, The Art of Pleasing at Court.* Provincial nobles, like the court aristocracy, found this literature indispensable when they instructed their children in the decorum that brought honor and esteem to their families. As generations were reared to seek distinction through education and civility, the culture of nobility became one of sophistication and cultivation, displacing to some extent the previously dominant culture of valor.

TASTE AND FASHION

Embedded in these developing concepts of civility and *honnêteté* was the seventeenth-century idea of taste. Michael Moriarity writes that "'taste' mattered in all of this because it could be represented as, essentially, the knowledge that pertains to *honnetêté,* and that distinguishes the *honnête homme* and his female counterpart from the popular masses and everything that smacks of their way of life."[10] Taste and *honnêteté* worked in tandem to distinguish the nobleman or noblewoman and clearly separated them from those below. The Chevalier de Méré, the seventeenth-century author and theorist, clarified the relationship by maintaining that "taste is the knowledge, more strictly the effect of knowledge, presupposed by *honnêteté.*"[11]

Many bourgeois families possessed the financial means to purchase titles of nobility and maintain great estates, but these acquisitions did not offer proof of taste. For some intellectuals taste was a quality present from birth. One period voice, Saint-Evremond, articulated especially clearly the innate quality of taste and emphasized its appearance in those of social and cultural hegemony.[12] Commenting on the exclusive and innate nature of taste, he wrote to urge a sympathy toward those less fortunate ones whom nature had not graced with such competitive advantage: "That which we call Taste is a figurative sense, is a very rare thing, and but very few people can boast of it. 'Tis scarce to be learnt or taught, but it must be born with us. Exquisite Knowledge seems to be above it, and carries a greater latitude: but in the commerce of the world, and in most affairs of life, a good Taste is, in truth, of equal service, and it acts its part very well. When we have got this advantage, we ought not to run down those that have it not. We have no demonstration to convince our opponents, and shew them that they are in the wrong. 'Tis easier to bring them over to our side by insinuation and address, than to persuade them by arguments."[13]

Saint-Evremond associated taste not only with elites but specifically with court society. For him politeness was indeed the product of court society because it was an essential prerequisite that enabled courtiers to please the prince. In contrast, he observed, towns and republics require that men work for a living, rather than serve as pleasing and polite sycophants, and were therefore left no time or energy for the art of pleasing, the lack of which made them "more clownish."[14]

The seventeenth-century origins of the concept of taste also included the appearance of a new style of cooking and the cookbooks that inspired and guided it. A later chapter will address the impact of these books on dining and aristocratic sociability, but it is important to consider here their role in shaping the concept of good taste and assigning it to the nobility. Taste had traditionally been viewed as very individual, a "kind of sympathy between a person's nature and a particular food, and dislikes resulted from physiological aversion."[15] This interpretation began to give way in midcentury to a more Platonic notion that put forward the idea of "good taste," a universal quality that, in the view of cookbook authors, resided in France within its elites. Even as a developing literature shaped the culinary discourse on taste, the concept was in no way restricted to food. Indeed, the idea of good taste in the arts and other matters developed alongside and often served as a metaphor for culinary taste.[16] The association of taste with the nobility in particular and elites in general continued into the eighteenth century. Enlightenment intellectuals wrestled with the meaning of taste, and though some aesthetic theory advanced its universality, other intellectuals and commentators still argued that good taste was exclusive to the upper-class milieu.[17] Even as eighteenth-century aesthetic theory held out the possibility that good taste could occur at any level of society, most intellectuals who entered this debate acknowledged the fact that upper class society was more likely to produce people of taste.[18]

Ideas of taste and refinement figured prominently in the period debate commonly referred to as the battle between the ancients and the moderns. As French thinkers reflected on civilized values and norms, they discussed politeness, civility, and *honnêteté* as foundations of refinement. It was clear to them that refinement and taste were class based and had achieved their fullest modern development in a particular nation. They considered France and its elites the true repositories of taste and the aesthetic good judgment that accompanied it.[19]

According to many French intellectuals, good taste, then, was much more likely to be found in elite society and in France, which, not surprisingly, was equally hospitable to its twin—though sometimes antithetical— concept, fashion. Here was implied a certain genius, a certain sense of style that existed only at the top echelons. In this way fashion and taste were inextricably linked and of special significance in the reign of Louis XIV, when both acted as important social markers. In her study of the origins of French style, Joan DeJean asserts that during this reign France came to be viewed as the source of fashion. "France [had] acquired a sort of monopoly on culture, style, and luxury living, a position that it has occupied ever since."[20] She argues that the cultivation of a French style was specifically a matter of government policy and that Louis XIV was directly involved in the formulation of such policy and its modes of implementation, with oversight to a large extent by the famous architect of mercantilism, Colbert. Economic historians have written at great length about the mercantilist policies of Colbert and specifically noted his efforts to associate France with luxury and quality. Commentators on material culture and the decorative arts also view this period as the beginning of French ascendancy in matters of style and fashion. In describing the crown's role in transforming France into the nation that dominated the production of luxury products and that defined trends in fashion, Leora Auslander argues that "France competed in the strategic world economy and polity through its aesthetic prowess." Much of this momentum she attributes to royal policies designed to "push French furniture to new heights so as to reinforce its power abroad as well as at home."[21]

Ultimately, the motor that sustained fashion was the rise of modern consumerism. With consumerism came the purchase of luxuries on a previously unparalleled scale. Since the Renaissance, the use of luxuries and exotic goods had distinguished European elites by offering tangible evidence of their taste and connoisseurship. In this way, luxuries marked social rank. In the early seventeenth century, many European markets were inundated by a profusion of consumer goods, a fact that was celebrated and depicted by the Dutch still-life painters.[22] "It was luxury production that supplied the elites with the markers of their status and authority, and that embodied the definitions of refinement of taste, elegance of design and power of expression."[23] Goods of great value marked their owners' social status and constituted a basis of social power. John Shovlin describes luxury goods as a contemporary "theatre of power" and depicts the process of *représentation,* or the effort to create an aura around those in power by the use of material display. By the late seventeenth century, luxury goods were essential means of communicating and maintaining social and political power. But Shovlin makes clear that goods did more than communicate; they not only signified a certain quality but actually assisted in forming that quality.[24] By 1700, consumption of luxury goods extended well beyond the ranks of elites to include a much wider spectrum of the European population. The pursuit of upward social mobility spurred acquisitiveness as families sought to emulate the lifestyle of their superiors. But simple emulation alone does not explain the trend.[25] Consumer choices were governed also by fashion and changing styles.

Writing about clothing, Daniel Roche maintains that fashion appreciation extended into even the rural societies of ancien régime France and that fashionable or modish dress reflected a society that at many levels valued change and novelty and understood obsolescence.[26] As a means of distinguishing oneself or one's family, according to Roche, clothes were "employed to erect a barrier, to stave off the pressure of imitators and followers who must be kept at a distance, and who always lagged behind in some nuance in the choice of color or way of tying a ribbon or cravat."[27] Jean-Baptiste Morvan de Bellegarde commented on the ephemeral nature of fashion and the French attachment to it: "Every *New Fashion* has something shocking in it at first 'till the Imagination is accustomed to it by Use. It is the Novelty however, . . . , that is the only Merit of a *Fashion;* the *French* will not allow any thing to be *agreable* [*sic*], but what is New; they are weary of seeing the same Objects; and, being naturally of a lively and impatient Temper, are soon tired with what they were most fond of before; from whence that Eagerness proceeds of running into *New Fashions;* without considering whether they in the least contributed to Ornament or Conveniency."[28]

The pervasive influence of *la mode* provoked quick reaction and fierce debate by moralists of the period. François de Grenaille complained to La Bruyère that fashion "reigned everywhere, in Paris and in the provinces, it imposes itself on everyone, from master to valet, it regulates everything, from dress to gardens, from buildings to dishes, in language as in the written word; nothing can stop it, not even religion."[29] Fitelou argued that, thanks to fashion, objects had strayed from their original function, a change regrettable on a number of levels. Clothing, for instance, no longer conformed to the natural laws of necessity, *honnêteté,* frugality, *commodité,* and distinction (marking social rank).[30] Fashion sabotaged the very social markers and class distinctions it was meant to define; it generated social ambiguity, and it enabled people to violate the natural order. He adumbrated the idea of fashion slavery when he described its followers as laboring under a self-imposed yoke.[31]

Fitelou and his fellow critics likened *la mode* to an infection resulting from the germ of original sin. Susceptibility to fashion trends was clearly rooted in gender, particularly the weakness of women ever since Eve. These men blamed women for the problem and offered as evidence for their position the fickle and mercurial nature of fashion. For Fitelou and Grenaille, women first fell prey to fashion and then exposed their husbands and sons. Such gendering was not limited to fashion critics; even Donneau de Visé, the editor of *Le Mercure galant* and a reporter on fashion's trends who advised elite audiences what they needed to purchase in order to be *à la mode,* made it clear that fashion was feminine. According to Jennifer Jones, his manner was not critical; he simply pointed out the less serious nature of fashion when compared with more masculine endeavors such as war. Naturally, then, the news of fashion was spread first and foremost through a crucial communication network of women.[32]

Regardless of the positions taken on the social and moral effects of fashion, all who wrote on the topic recognized its essential Frenchness. Jones concludes, "Although this deceptive goddess [fashion] unsettled gender, class, and political relations and identities, even her harshest critics were clear that she could not be banished from the kingdom altogether; for *la mode* was not simply a deity, she was a French deity."[33]

By the 1660s the association of fashion with Frenchness held wide sway in French culture and society. The French saw themselves as intrinsically fashionable; people in foreign lands certainly regarded them as trendsetters, for better or worse. To outsiders, given the fundamentally protean nature of fashion, it followed that the French as a people exhibited fickleness, a proclivity and fondness for change. Acknowledging this tendency, *Le Mercure* identified the root cause of this national characteristic as boredom, a boredom that necessitated perpetual change, even to the extent of wearing clothes that were less attractive or less flattering to the individual. In this awareness of national character, Jones argues, we see the basis for the royal policy of promoting luxury trade. In short, the internal campaign to sell French helped to promote the idea that there was something innately fashionable in all things French.[34] Though foreigners have observed and remarked on the French talent for fashion since the seventeenth century, perhaps the editor of *Le Mercure* himself expressed it best in a spirit of pride and boosterism: "Everyone must agree . . . that nothing pleases more than fashions born in France, and that all that is made there has a certain look that foreigners cannot give to their goods, even when they surpass French goods in beauty."[35] This perception, that no one can dress like the French, took hold under Louis XIV and has been reinvented generationally ever since.

Le Mercure was also deeply aware that at its most fundamental level fashionability was an attribute that applied to elites. Certainly, the magazine addressed French elites. It described trends at court and among the *grands seigneurs,* which served to inspire in turn noble families below them and in the provinces, with the tacit acknowledgment that as soon as fashion was too widely adopted it passed out of vogue. This impressed readers with the need to stay on top of their game, understanding the ephemeral nature of style and accepting the importance of fashion in distinguishing noblemen and noblewomen from the bourgeoisie.[36]

Taste, fashion, and the desire for distinction or separateness also guided consumer choices in other categories of goods, including furniture, tableware, and household textiles. For historian Natasha Coquery, consumption of luxurious household goods had become by the eighteenth century an essential means by which French aristocrats distinguished themselves. As the court aristocracy became a sort of useless "caste ornamentale," consumption served to set it apart as an exclusive social category.[37] Michel Figeac has written about similar patterns of consumption among nobles in the province of Guyenne. He too found that in the eighteenth century provincial nobles invested heavily in furnishings and interior decoration.[38] By their acquisition of goods, noble families strived to communicate, indeed clarify, their position for the rest of society. Katie Scott describes their relationship with consumer goods: "Once nobility ceased to be a matter of action and became a question of station, noblemen were necessarily compelled to distinguish the 'place' by multiplying the visual symbols of rank, thus overlaying and reinforcing (with the help of newly fashioned rules of decorum) the judicial divisions between social groups and perceptual markers, so that each estate appeared like 'a nation within the Nation'; a commonwealth with its own laws, customs, language and culture."[39] Through their tasteful and stylish acquisitions, what distinguished the nobility from the others was made abundantly clear.

Other reasons for the ruling class's investment in fashion and luxuries, not as obvious to the modern reader for whom conspicuous consumption and retail therapy are a sine qua non, have been considered by sociologists and historians for some time. The grand old thesis of consumption was that of Thorstein Veblen, who at the end of the nineteenth century first wrote about competition and emulation as driving forces in the acquisition of nonessential goods, an interpretation commonly known as the Veblen thesis and resting on the principle of status consumption.[40] A few years later the German sociologist Werner Sombart looked to psychology and human sexuality to explain the acquisition of luxurious goods, which he argued stemmed from basic desire for gratification of the senses. In his effort to understand the forces that drove court society, the sociologist Norbert Elias advanced the argument that these goods were essential to courtiers and aristocrats because they allowed them to assert their rank within elite society.[41] Much more recently historians, in looking at the actual goods that elites acquired, have tried explain the growth of the luxury market in terms that add more layers of complexity to consumption as a historical force. For example, in a beautifully detailed study of luxury production and consumption in France since the reign of Louis XIV, Auslander has argued that the design of furniture became a tool of the state, with the patronage of *ébénistes* and craftsmen to furnish Versailles, and, by extension, the homes of aristocrats, all serving to project the power of the absolutist state.[42] Other historians have preferred to emphasize the importance of taste in cultural rather than political terms. In his study of the consumption of art in Renaissance Italy, Richard Goldthwaite maintains that the purchase of luxuries served to define a household as one of taste, an idea central to the cultural identity of elite families. The dynamics were complex. In short, this was no simple matter of conspicuous consumption.[43]

As the world of nobles evolved from a warrior culture to one based on ideas of pedigree, taste, and fashion, their residences changed dramatically. Peter Thornton offers a description of the medieval residence and the transition that took place in the early modern period:

> This unsettled way of life among the seigneurial class dictated the form of furnishings that a great lord would take with him as he moved from one castle to the next, or from house to house. Some rugged pieces of furniture of no great value will have remained at each place, ready for use, but the more important furnishings had to be mobile, they had to be capable of being packed onto a cart in the baggage train, and set forth again at the next place of sojourn. Tapestries, that could be rolled up, and folding chairs met this requirement admirably; so did the trestle-tables, folding beds and cushions. Hangings that could be used to transform a bare hall into an impressive setting for ceremony, a cosy bower or a charming bedchamber were likewise particularly in demand.
>
> By the seventeenth century all this had changed. . . . Their houses remained furnished all the time. . . . Most of the old forms of furniture thus became obso-

lete. Tapestries and folding chairs happened to retain their importance as status symbols but no longer had any practical value; as for the rest, they were supplanted by new forms of furniture which were evolved to suit the new, static circumstances—the massive bed, the elaborate buffet, the writing-cabinet on a stand and the draw-table, for example. That these lost their massive character and became more delicate and graceful during the seventeenth century had to do with aesthetics and notions of comfort, and hardly at all with practical considerations.[44]

What exactly to buy? What were the stylish goods, the fashionable furnishings that would turn the home of a noble family from simply a large castle, spartan in its contents, into a dwelling that showcased abundant fashionable, tasteful, and magnificent items? Answers to these questions ensured that the medieval residence bore little resemblance to its seventeenth-century successor.

How did provincial nobles know what to buy, where to buy it, and how to use it? Crucial in the process of acquisition and change was the emergence of publications that promoted the development of a French style. This was the primary medium for the spread of a French style, both to the provinces and to England and other parts of the Continent. Provincial nobles, particularly the great provincial families, visited Paris, and some were entertained in the stylish *hôtels* of the Parisian aristocracy. Once they saw homes decorated in the latest trends and to spectacular effect, the desire to adopt Parisian designs must have been irresistible, and those who had been to Paris surely took home inspiration and some practical knowhow. But historians of interior decoration maintain that it was publications that were the major medium through which design ideas radiated from Paris. Genre scenes, including the work of Abraham Bosse, offered detailed information about how Parisian elites lived and decorated their homes. And, of course, there were the great architectural works of the period including Louis Savot's *L'Architecture françoise des batimens particuliers*. First published in 1624, Savot's book was reissued in 1673 and widely circulated. It was replete with practical information to assist the reader in carrying out French design principles.

Those decorating an existing residence found countless ideas in the engravings that circulated around Paris from the 1630s. Thornton describes their proliferation as astonishing. For inspiration architects and artisans consulted engravings "devoted to a particular class of ornament or feature—panelling, doors, chimneypieces, ceilings, candle stands, tables, bed-alcoves, frames, vases, and every other sort of ornamental detail."[45] They were sold singly or in sets, and Thornton argues that they were a treasure trove of information featuring architectural detail presented in a larger, completely appointed scene. "For example, the designs for a chimneypiece might show the latest form of the fire-dog as well; there might also be a *garniture* of vases or a clock on the mantel-shelf, and the opening of the fireplace might be fitted with a decorated chimney-board."[46]

Later in the seventeenth century, fashion plates served the same purpose. In depicting a fashionable nobleman or noblewoman decked out in the latest Parisian styles, the artist also situated him or her in a setting that was strictly *à la mode*.[47] No single publication was more important in fashionable circles than *Le Mercure gallant*. First published in 1672 by Jean Donneau de Visé, this periodical covered literature, court gossip, and fashion. Although much of his interest in fashion centered on clothing, de Visé also reported on furnishings and interior decoration, and his targeted audience was the French nobility, or *"gens de qualité."*[48]

Among the fashionable consumers who read *Le Mercure* were provincial nobles with lives significantly removed from those epicenters of style, Versailles and Paris. Figeac has studied the homes and consumption patterns of noble families in Guyenne, and his work with notary inventories reveals remarkable similarities in the consumption patterns of that group with those of the noble families examined in this study. Tapestries and wall hangings were dominant elements of the décors of elite homes, and the affordable Bergamo tapestries were especially popular in both places. The noble families in Guyenne also shared a fondness for Turkish rugs to serve as table covers. Walls were adorned with a similar array of paintings, portraits, and engravings, and they chose to decorate according to the same color schemes. Figeac found that the interiors of urban residences in the late seventeenth century were generally rather austere compared with those of the late eighteenth century, with the impulse to accumulate revealed increasingly and especially in the homes of the presidents of the Parlement.[49]

The interiors of the châteaux in the Bordeaux region varied predictably in scale but not in the nature of their contents or basic decorative elements, and they paralleled significantly those found in Dauphiné. Though located at different points along the periphery of the realm, the nobilities of each province had begun by the reign of Louis XIV to participate in essentially the same consumer culture, one in which individual choices were driven by fashion and markets. National and international trends of fashion came to replace the more traditional and regionally based material culture of earlier centuries. Why were France's provincial nobilities, so proud of their regional identity and often fiercely opposed to centralization, so easily seduced by the styles and tastes emanating from Versailles and Paris? An examination of the nobility of Dauphiné and its response to the emerging national market, consumerism, and fashion trends, viewed in a local social and political context, may help to answer this intriguing question.

Nobles in Dauphiné were a mixed group, consisting of traditional or warrior nobles, judges, and attorneys; yet they produced and embraced a homogeneous, if not a national, style. At the same time that the culture of the larger French nobility was evolving to one of civility and connoisseurship, the nobility of Dauphiné experienced a major assault from below, precipitating a political and social crisis that anticipated the antinoble ideas and initiatives of the French Revolution. Starting with its assault on the noble privilege of exemption from taxation, the Third Estate actually launched an attack that grew into a larger campaign against the nobility itself. Spokesmen for the Third Estate challenged the nobility's right to exemption as no longer valid because the nobility had ceased to perform its traditional military role. Moreover, they advanced the idea that in shirking their military responsibilities and behaving poorly in many other ways the nobility acted with utter indifference to the public good. What led to this great eruption of social conflict in Dauphiné?

POLITICS: THE *PROCÈS DES TAILLES*

Dauphiné was an important province at the outer reaches of the realm with a unique institutional history. By the terms of its transfer to the French crown in 1349, the province was guaranteed a substantial degree of autonomy and self-governance through its provincial assemblies and exemption from direct taxation. Over time and with the rising costs of war, the French crown chose to overlook the original agreement and to impose direct forms of taxation. The taille would be paid, but in what form? At the heart of the issue was the method of assessment, whether it would be levied against nonnoble individuals (*taille personnelle*) or nonnoble property (*taille reélle*). If the latter, nobles were liable to pay taxes on their nonfeudal property. To avoid this, the nobility of Dauphiné assiduously insisted that the tax should be personal, tied to an individual's status as a commoner, and that nobles should be exempt, as was true for most of France, in compensation for the personal sacrifices nobles made defending the realm.[50]

The question soon turned on a determination of the legitimacy of the claims to nobility on the part of those seeking exemption from taxation. As elsewhere in France, Dauphiné had seen growing numbers of families engaged in upward social mobility. Their claims to nobility, and therefore to tax exemption, became a hotly debated issue as the taxation controversy unfolded. When a noble, no matter how recently ennobled, acquired nonnoble or nonfeudal property, that property was exempted from assessment. This decreased the amount of available taxable land and increased the burden on the rest of the villages and urban communities, which remained responsible for producing the full tax amount. To lessen this burden, leaders of the Third Estate advanced the case for personal taxation, which would have compelled nobles to pay taxes on nonfeudal acquisitions.[51]

In the debate over the nature of the taille, then, the alienation of land by nobility became a particular bone of contention. It appears that, accounting for sixteenth-century demographic attrition and inflation, the nobility remained large enough and prosperous enough to dominate the land market. Daniel Hickey argues that the old families of Dauphiné survived the inflation of the sixteenth century in secure, if not prime, financial condition. Some extinction of old lines had taken place, but at a lower rate than the average for other parts of France. Above all, older families were the most active in the late sixteenth-century land market, both buying and selling seigniories. Their territorial possessions stand in contrast to the much more modest holdings of the new nobility. This leads Hickey to conclude that the financial position of the old nobility had not been challenged by "enriched *anoblis*."[52] Certainly, speculation in land imposed a greater tax burden on nonnobles, and this fact focused the general debate on noble investments, all elevating the overall level of discord.

A close examination of the social contours of the conflict shows that at its heart it set in opposition the nobility and the elite of the Third Estate. Hickey has argued persuasively that urban elites were the element of the Third Estate most affected by taxation and the reduction in taxable land, and the bourgeois elite of Grenoble, Valence, and Romans were the most heavily taxed social element within their respective towns. In Grenoble, for example, the legal professionals represented 14 percent of those taxed, and their share amounted to 23 percent of the taxes paid; merchants paid 11 percent, and bourgeois investors another 12 percent. The bourgeois elite were most affected by the tax structure as it currently existed, and they had the most to gain if the nobility was taxed on its nonnoble holdings.[53]

Adding to the disaffection of the bourgeois elites was the fact that their social and professional worlds were essentially the same as those occupied by recently ennobled families, whose exemption from the tax rolls increased the burden on everyone else. They lived in the same quarters; they worked in many of the same professions; their lifestyles were entirely similar. As Hickey has pointed out, very little separated the two groups except the fact that one paid the taille and the other did not.[54]

Still, noble status and exemption from taxation carried more than simple financial benefit. Social distinction and privilege resulting from ennoblement certainly set these two groups, though living in close proximity, worlds apart. And by a decision of the crown in 1602,[55] future access to the nobility was drastically limited for Grenoble's jurists.[56] Now, in a city of sovereign courts, judicial elites confronted new institutional obstacles. Not that ennoblement had always been easy for attorneys and their families. Historically they had been frustrated by the fact that in Dauphiné it was always easier for a family to be ennobled by military service, a circumstance that undoubtedly resulted from the frontier location of the province. At the crossroads of the conflict in sixteenth-century Italy, the Dauphinois were deeply involved in the Habsburg-Valois Wars. And it was these conflicts, along with the Wars of Religion, that offered many families opportunities for ennoblement and enrichment.[57] Hickey points out a number of cases in which jurists who later took up arms were ennobled only after and in rec-ognition of their achievements on the battlefield, suggesting that the most rapid way to *anoblissement* was through military service.[58] Unquestionably, this privileging of military careers coupled with the restrictions on enno-blement after 1602 acted to exclude many talented Dauphinois jurists and their families from the social privilege that in another province would have been open to them. Educated and ambitious, they became potent spokes-people for the case of the Third Estate in its struggle to achieve fairness in the matter of taxation.

To aid their respective cases, the two sides constructed legal and his-torical arguments, trying their utmost to create an atmosphere of favorable public opinion. A paper trail of pamphlets and legal documents was created that enables the historian to discern the details of the issue and to probe the systems of values and the social identities associated with the two sides. Each constructed identities that relied on achievement; each referred to acquired characteristics and talked in terms of self-fashioning. The nobility, which traditionally relied so heavily on the idea of virtue through inheri-tance, even stressed ambition and the idea of professional success. Jona-than Dewald maintains that by the seventeenth century the ambition and success of the nobleman had become paramount in defining his personal identity and contributing to his sense of self-worth.[59] Thus, achieved sta-tus was a cultural concept that swayed early modern imaginations because society, albeit still a society of orders, made possible advancement through achievement. Self-presentation and material consumption became essen-tial means of creating distinction. Furthermore, both sides used the lan-guage of achievement and ambition because their attorneys were spokes-men for that growing culture. They belonged to families that through their own efforts at self-construction and self-presentation had pursued upward social mobility, some with greater success than others, but success defined them all. Envy, emulation, and the desire for distinction were basic to the whole affair, as they constituted motive forces in the social world of self-construction.

The case for the Third Estate was made by attorneys like Claude Dela-grange. He argued that nobles were undeserving of tax exemption because their military contributions to the province and the realm were minimal and highly exaggerated. Others reiterated this message and went even further. They raised questions about the virtue of a nobility that exhibited utter indifference to the suffering of the people, and they challenged the noble claims of illegitimate children and children of tax-exempt officials.[60]

Representatives for the Third Estate presented their case in patently political terms. Central to their rhetoric were two related ideas: the notion of the public good (*le bien public*) and the concept of *la patrie*. Proclaiming an ideal of devotion to the public good, they charged that the nobility's claims to immunity from the taille ran contrary to the welfare of the state.[61] Apparent in this rhetoric is a nascent sense of community or patriotism.[62] How deeply this feeling ran is debatable. It is significant, however, that those writing on behalf of the Third Estate made effective use of a nationalist and patriotic discourse imbued with all its attendant emotions. The Third Estate existed as a community with shared interests, part of a nation with a common foe—the nobility. By advancing the cause of *la patrie*, the Third Estate offered the monarchy a weapon that it might use against provincial nobles who resisted taxation—the interest of the nation, the community, a concept that was not imposed from the center on the periphery but rather sprang from the social conflicts of the periphery.[63]

Antoine Rambaud argued so vociferously that the nobility contributed nothing to the public or community as to speculate that the world would be a happier place without it. He wrote that only the greater nobles, the *seigneurs de marque*, actually fulfilled the military obligation that entitled them to exemption from the taille. It was the rest of the nobles, the majority, who shamelessly never wanted to leave their homes. Rambaud drew a clear distinction, then, between older families that served the community and more recently ennobled houses that acted selfishly and were therefore the real targets of his vitriole.[64]

By making this distinction between the older nobility and the *anoblis* claiming noble exemption, Rambaud drew upon the contempt with which the urban elite in particular regarded those families that had only recently been recognized as noble. This was the group whose exemptions had increased the burden on the Third Estate, and this was the group about which they had the most disparaging things to say.[65] Rambaud took the culture of nobility and the arguments launched by the attorneys for the nobility and turned them back as a weapon against it. Much of the nobility's case was based on the idea that military service and sacrifice for the community exempted it from taxation; yet Rambaud argued that many nobles never served and never left home. By singling out the *anoblis* and reserving praise for the older and greater nobility, Rambaud's pamphlet brought the nature of this social conflict into clearer focus.

If the Third Estate won its case, most *parlementaires* would be adversely affected. At the end of the sixteenth century, the Parlement of Dauphiné was a court populated by a mixed group. Particularly relevant to the *procès* were individuals in the process of claiming nobility and its most coveted privilege. According to Maurice Virieux, who has studied the social composition of the Parlement between 1596 and 1635, a full 26 percent of the officers were attempting to claim nobility but remained on unstable ground.[66] Approximately 10 percent of its members had established nobility only as recently as the late sixteenth century.[67] In the whole province, 107 households were ennobled during the period 1587–1634. The amount of potentially taxable property held by these families was enormous. These *anoblis* were the most vulnerable because the Third Estate in its various appeals and pamphlets focused particularly on the recently ennobled and families in the process of claiming nobility. To the Third Estate, they constituted the real enemy. The villains of its polemics, these were the same families with whom the Third Estate elite shared quarters and lifestyles and the very families that inspired particular contempt.[68]

So only in the most superficial way was the *procès des tailles* a conflict between noble and commoner. It was fundamentally a competition between those who had recently succeeded in claiming nobility with its attendant honors and those who had not yet managed to do the same. Nor was this conflict simply a matter of envy; there was no doubt that the advantages gained by the recently ennobled added to the tax burden suffered by those who had not managed to achieve noble status. Little wonder the groups' familiarity was attended with such mutual contumely and disdain.[69]

In 1634 the conflict over taxation was resolved by a simple chronological compromise. The older nobility established for itself an immunity not extended to those people ennobled after 1602. For recent *anoblis*, their victory was the retention of their noble status, and in this sense the settlement imparted an important concession to them as well. Tax exemption was not the only privilege of nobility; there remained juridical privileges and other honors conferred on noble families in a society where privilege attached to rank. But not only did the attack on the nobility, especially its most recently ennobled families, anticipate by almost two centuries the universalist rhetoric of the French Revolution; it was also devastatingly critical of the provincial nobility. The attorneys of the Third Estate had challenged the basis for the nobility's privileged status and had pointedly controverted its claims to distinction.

The *procès des tailles* evinced how different Dauphinois tax structures and nobilities were compared with those of neighboring Provence and nearby Languedoc. For Hickey, proximity to these two provinces of the *taille réelle* made the *taille personnelle* of Dauphiné seem all the more unfair.[70] In contrast to Provence, where the local nobility included many recently ennobled *parlementaire* families, that of Dauphiné would not. Dauphiné did not experience this crucial social evolution. With significantly fewer jurists successful in their efforts at ennoblement, the nobility of Dauphiné was deprived of vital legal talent. The attorneys who so successfully represented the Third Estate might well have been advocates for the Second Estate had avenues for ennoblement been more available.[71]

Having survived this assault on aristocratic privilege and honor, the nobles of Dauphiné no doubt felt themselves in a different social world. As damage control, they confronted the urgent need to reconstruct and maintain perceptions of their esteem and honor. In this context, quality and opulence of lifestyle took on greater meaning, especially for families ennobled after 1602. They had endured the Third Estate's challenges to their claims to nobility but had lost their tax-exempt status; how best now to communicate the qualities that separated them from the rest of society? The pursuit of material culture was an option. In this context of social conflict and horizontal solidarities, lifestyle assumed greater importance to those families, especially *anoblis*. Now their honor and esteem stemmed in even greater measure from the wealth that marked a noble lifestyle. Society attached signal importance to all relevant characteristics of aristocratic life: ambition, self-construction, *politesse, honnêteté,* education, connoisseurship, distinction, and consumption. These markers existed in an increasingly elaborate and exotic material world, and they required money. Their cultivation required levels of income that set nobles apart from the rest of society.

The French nobility as a whole regarded consumption as an essential tool in generating an aura of distinctiveness. Nobles' spending power, consumer choices, and sense of fashion demonstrated how different they were from those beneath them. In short, the world of goods became the world of nobility. And in Dauphiné, the world of goods became even more vital as nobles struggled to redeem and to redefine themselves in their own eyes and in the eyes of their local community.

Where did the Dauphinois buy these goods? Some items came from Paris, and in rare instances the notaries who inventoried the households identified goods as Parisian. But almost never was the provenance of a item discussed, and we can only guess that most belongings were purchased from artisans and shops in Grenoble or Lyons. Dauphiné's location at a trading crossroads provided it with access to markets in Lyons, Geneva, Provence, Italy, and ultimately Paris.[72] Lyons would have been the closest market of significance, and the economy of Lyons rested on its textile industry. As a result, it was a major producer of luxury silks, and the designs its weavers turned out were inspired by the fashionable consumer in Paris. This was true of the eighteenth century and probably of the seventeenth as well. Studies of silk production and the luxury market of eighteenth-century Lyons have established the existence of a close design relationship between producers in Lyons and consumers in Paris, showing that the *marchands merciers* of Paris worked rather closely with merchants and manufacturers in Lyons to innovate and produce designs that would appeal to the fashion-conscious Parisian constumer.[73] This sort of "design dialogue" would have inevitably meant that designs inspired by Paris were available to customers in Lyons and other nearby locales.

By choosing to accentuate the French style, and by demonstrating their sheer ability to consume, Dauphinois noble families living on the periphery sought to clarify and justify their rank for the rest of provincial society. As consumers, these Dauphinois families were participants in the emergence of an elite French national culture. They distinguished themselves by their choices and purchases, and these were driven by the same fashions and styles that prevailed in other and distant communities. In this way was formed what T. H. Breen has called the "standardization of the market-place." He writes about the American colonists, and he argues that their consumer experiences served to unite scattered populations and "to perceive, however dimly, the existence of an 'imagined community.'"[74] This standardization was occurring in France as well, in a distant culture and different society. The market was transforming Dauphinois elites and connecting them to a national and even international community of elites.

Anthropologists who study consumption and culture maintain that material possessions can serve to clarify social relationships.[75] Through their possessions and choices, families communicated more than wealth and spending power; they communicated their rank within society. Consumption existed, therefore, as a means of communication. For Pierre Bourdieu, "it presupposes practical mastery of a cipher or code."[76] Its mastery distinguished the connoisseur for his or her "cultural competence." In this way, recently ennobled Dauphinois, with a need to set themselves apart from the social elements from which they sprang and more securely establish themselves within the social milieu to which they aspired, were distinguished in part by cultural competency. But their consumer choices were no simple matter of imitation or emulation. By the late seventeenth century, cultural competency was being defined in part by the market and the desire to be on top of fashion.

Finally, local social trends as well as national political forces may have affected the adoption and spread of the French style and other forms of consumption in this remote province that traditionally heralded its regional privileges and local identity. In Dauphiné the pressure to *vivre noblement* may have been particularly intense because provincials had spent the first half of the century battling issues of noble claims and privilege. I do not argue that the *procès des tailles* and the policies of central government were solely responsible for the adoption of a French style or for the tendency toward more conspicuous forms of consumption. I do put forward the recognition that in the material culture and social world of provincial nobles we see, at least faintly, the galvanizing hand of the state and, more clearly, the power of the market and modern consumerism. In the end, the acquisitions of certain goods point to the successful reception of an important aspect of French culture, interior decoration, in a region whose local customs and unique institutional history had earlier set nobility in opposition to the crown. By the middle of the eighteenth century, foreign consumers regarded France as the trendsetter, and style was increasingly associated with the French national identity. Being French, with the fashionability and taste that implied, became a mark of distinction for provincial nobles, not only in Dauphiné but throughout the realm.

LE LUXE

SPLENDOR AND LUXURY

How exactly did material culture define elite society at the frontier of France? Interior decoration had played a major role in defining European elites since the period of the Renaissance. This was nothing new. Interiors provided a medium for conspicuous consumption as elites filled their households with expensive, decorative, and exotic items, and by their consumer choices they demonstrated their fashion sensibility. It was in Italy that magnificence and splendor first became the standards for the residences of elites,[1] a standard that eventually extended to France and its provincial nobilities. By the seventeenth century the furnishings of châteaux and urban townhouses had become significantly more elaborate than in previous centuries because the interior of the home came to assume ever greater importance to the family. It offered concrete evidence of a family's wealth, station, taste, and refinement.

What did magnificence and splendor mean? According to Richard Goldthwaite, the idea of magnificence was redefined in the Italian Renaissance so that it resonated with a nonfeudal society. Its basic meaning: "magnificence is the use of wealth in a way that manifests those qualities that express one's innate dignity, thereby establishing one's reputation by arousing the esteem and admiration of others."[2] As for splendor, it "expresses itself in the elegance and refinement with which one lives his life within buildings."[3] Essentially, splendor existed in tandem with magnificence, values established in Italy and later developed in northern Europe, and involved the consumption of luxury. While splendor referred to household furnishings, Italian humanists applied the concept of magnificence to architecture. Splendor was the effect, that is, the virtue that resided in a noble family with the means to acquire luxury goods and therefore to demonstrate its capacity for refinement.[4]

In a later chapter I will consider how concepts of luxury evolved and assumed new meanings, but the basic meaning of what had traditionally been deemed luxury, or what we might classify as the Old Luxury, remained essentially the same and was to a large extent the preserve of the ruling class. The seventeenth century saw fundamental changes in attitudes toward these goods. First, it witnessed what Christopher Berry calls the demoralization of luxury, or the gradual abandonment of the classical notion that associated luxury with desire and, therefore, corruption. This traditional view necessarily understood luxury in opposition to necessity, a binary relationship that was weakened by changing ideas about the former quality.[5] The shift in thinking about luxury did not occur overnight, and intellectuals continued to write about moral failures associated with luxury consumption well into the Enlightenment. Those who opposed acquisitiveness argued it was particularly problematic in the case of the nobility because luxury undermined its moral superiority. These conservative voices believed it natural for the bourgeoisie to engage in conspicuous consumption, and they viewed, by its efforts to promote the production of luxury, the monarchy as the accomplice of wealthy merchants.[6] Yet their reaction and opposition to the spending habits of noble families was tacit recognition that the culture of nobility was in transition. Moreover, others challenged this reactionary perspective. A number of seventeenth-century philosophers, economists, and political theorists began to rethink this relationship and argue that luxury could be good. Nicolas Barbon, among others, maintained that desire was natural rather than corrupting and that the desire for goods promoted economic growth and development. His was among the first stimulus, perhaps trickle-down, arguments in favor of luxury consumption.[7]

Barbon provided an intellectual rationale for the growing acquisition of luxuries in seventeenth-century England (and elsewhere). In a detailed study of luxury consumption in England, Linda Levy Peck asserts that the same began as early as the late sixteenth century and grew especially in the seventeenth century (and therefore changing ideas of luxury). One major point is that this occurred well before the eighteenth century, the period to which historians of material culture attribute the stimulus of modern consumerism. Writing about elites, Peck argues that English men and women purchased more and more luxuries because "the well-off increasingly identified themselves as cosmopolitan through the appropriation of continental luxuries. . . . They sought to share in a Western European culture which was expressed in what they read, how they lived, what they wore, where they went, what they built, and who they imagined themselves to be. New artifacts helped to craft reinvented identities."[8] By apposition, just as purchasing continental goods made English elites more cosmopolitan, the accumulation of foreign goods was essential to the construction of this new and international identity in France and elsewhere. As a rule, foreign goods were especially luxurious because they were precious. This was nothing new because foreign goods had long constituted luxury items and served to stimulate and inspire long-distance trade.[9] But goods did not need to be foreign to be luxurious. By the late seventeenth century, thanks in large part to Colbert, France had earned its reputation, both domestically and abroad, as the font of luxurious commodities.

What were the elements of luxury enjoyed by acquisition that defined noble households? Certain objects existed to communicate unambiguously ideas of taste, connoisseurship, and even family antiquity to the beholder. From one household to the next there was a predictable inventory of decorative items encoded with such meaning. Silver objects conveyed wealth and magnificence by their intrinsic value, but they also afforded opportunities to make claims, whether exaggerated or invented, about lineage and family antiquity because they were frequently engraved with the family coat of arms. And the family that possessed an extensive service of silver flatware and accessories usually seized the opportunity to distinguish them with its arms. Mary Douglas and Baron Isherwood have maintained that *sets* of objects, as opposed to single items, served categorically to indicate rank and status.[10] I will discuss silver services later.

Splendor extended beyond that which had intrinsic value to include that which had acquired value. Sculpture rarely appeared in the homes of these provincial nobles, but paintings were commonplace. By the second half of the century, many noble families could boast modest collections of paintings and the more affordable alternative, engravings. From the Renaissance, great art collections had been a foundation of Italian courtly splendor, and now the elite families in France regarded their collections as among their most valuable possessions. In fact, from the 1600s, collecting paintings became significantly more popular among elites, connected as it was to the emerging idea of *connoisseur*.[11] For inspiration they looked to the most prominent collectors of the realm. Although Louis XIII expressed little interest in accumulating art, Richelieu and Mazarin were two of the greatest collectors in France. Richelieu's personal collection encompassed 150 paintings, not including the many works he had commissioned by the most talented French artists. Later, Colbert encouraged Louis XIV to collect paintings and sculpture, which Louis did for a period; he became a more serious collector at the time of Colbert's death in 1683. Louis's real preference, however, was to exert artistic control by acting as patron and to spend the resources of the realm on architecture and interior decoration. Antoine Schnapper makes an important distinction between the roles of royal collector and royal patron, and he argues that art collections were only a secondary means of royal propaganda in seventeenth-century France and served at least until the 1680s as "accessories to buildings."[12]

Provincial elites may have regarded their art collections in similar fashion, or they may have valued them as some of their most treasured possessions. The fact that notaries were careful to describe subjects but never mention the artist by name suggests that this provincial art market was probably still in an early stage of development. The fact that notaries included the details of framing as well as the subject points to their awareness of the importance of the painting as a possession. This privileging of subject over artist was also true in sixteenth-century England, where elites built their art collections based on subject; it was only in the 1600s that collectors paid more serious attention to attribution and that the appreciation of particular artists became an indication of taste and refinement.[13] I submit that in provincial France attribution remained less important than subject until the eighteenth century. By far, and predictably, the most popular subjects in Dauphiné were religious in nature, and no collection failed to include some paintings devoted to the saints and the Crucifixion. But historical figures were also a common subject, especially portraits of the kings of France and some of the great ministers.

Portraits of ancestors and living family members also figured prominently in these collections and offered another means to display a distinguished lineage. Douglas and Isherwood include ancestral portraits in a class of designated "pure rank-markers."[14] Since these were commissioned works, portraits were likely to be a family's most expensive paintings.[15] In a society where antiquity and origins of family figured so prominently in the discourse about the privileges of nobility, portraits were treasured possessions. By hanging representations of themselves and their ancestors, families made bold statements about their wealth and pride, even as they did when they marked their silver with coats of arms.

A number of collections included still-life paintings, studies of flowers and fruit that celebrated not only the beauty of the objects but a culture of plenty. To relate to nature and foods as subjects for decorative purposes, to appreciate them for their aesthetic qualities, implied a privileged economic relationship with these items and a materially comfortable existence. The cultural and social meaning of the still-life painting has been the subject of debate in the past few decades, and interpretations vary widely. For some scholars the seventeenth-century tradition of still-life painting reflected a growing material obsession and acquisitiveness in which the subjects were chosen more for their appearance than for their moral value. Certainly, still-life has been associated with a lack of imagination. But other scholars take an opposite view and believe that the still-life tradition was inspired by the devotional beliefs expressed metaphorically through the subjects of the paintings. In particular, the great Dutch still-life tradition may have represented natural phenomena as a means of Christian expression.[16] Whatever the broader cultural meaning, still-life gained overall popularity in the seventeenth century and among noble families in Dauphiné.

Likewise, landscapes and seascapes appear increasingly over time in these inventories, in correspondence with the growing interest among French elites in landscape gardening. In her work on landscape design, Chandra Mukerji argues that gardening and landscaping, especially with exotic plants, were period forms of conspicuous consumption. An indication of wealth and taste, gardening was another form of material culture that could help to establish a family's position. And the landscape painting could serve as a model for the landscaped garden. Each represented ownership of landed property and a knowledge of the natural world that extended to the exotic.[17]

The exotic category of decorative elements gained in popularity through the seventeenth and eighteenth centuries. Among these, displayed both inside and outside, were shrubs that had been carefully trimmed and planted in large tubs or urns and in turn arranged in rows to decorate a long gallery or other large space. Orange trees, used to great effect at Versailles, were especially popular, and the interior space in which they were housed became known as an *orangerie*.[18] At Versailles the number of citrus trees reached three thousand; they were used not only outdoors in fair weather and in the Orangerie but also in the Hall of Mirrors and the king's apartments. Colbert and the design team that gathered such a large collection did so to satisfy the preferences of the king but also to demonstrate the power of the state; "controlling the plants from the Mediterranean in the vast Orangerie obliquely pointed to the ability of the French state to overcome the difficulties of distance and history, and govern this part of its territory."[19] Collections of orange trees were not common in Dauphiné, no doubt because of the hardship of maintaining them through an Alpine winter, but they did exist there.

This developing taste for the exotic was also expressed in the ownership of Turkish rugs, which, in almost every case, were employed as table covers. In the early seventeenth century Europeans began to display Turkish rugs as "table carpets" because they were too valuable to place on the floor. Certainly, the table carpet was de rigueur and even a dominant element of the well-appointed home. The demand for Anatolian rugs was so great that they were manufactured on a large scale expressly for export to Europe. Rugs from the Ottoman Empire also had the advantage of being generally smaller and more affordable than most Persian rugs.[20] By the late seventeenth century, families were choosing to locate more of their rugs on the floor in order to reveal the marquetry designs that had become a popular decorative feature on the surfaces of their tables.[21] Turkish rugs remained popular, and many households in Dauphiné had several, one for each room in which they received guests. By the end of the 1600s Turkish rugs appear to have receded somewhat in importance and popularity.

The other great textile furnishing was the wall hanging, and its most celebrated and costly form, the tapestry. Tapestries had long existed and served a very practical purpose, and, in addition to insulating a drafty room, they provided a dominant element of its décor. These woven tableaux could depict scenes or histories, or they could display a family's coat of arms or masses of foliage (*verdure* tapestries). Often they were simply woven into geometric designs. Especially common in Dauphiné were the more affordable *tapisseries de Bergame,* which often came in panels joined to create a larger piece. These were made of wool, consisting of coarsely woven designs of repetitive patterns (rather than pictorial subjects) such as the pomegranate or flame-stitch *point d'Hongerie* (a chevron pattern). Originally they were made in Italy, but in 1622 an Italian craftsman obtained permission to establish a shop in Lyons, where he manufactured the same style of textiles.[22] Lyons's close proximity to Grenoble and Dauphiné made these tapestries more affordable in the region. Other cities in France, such as Rouen, would also attempt to capitalize on the popularity of Bergamo-style tapestry.[23] In addition to these more commonplace hangings, some families owned the more valuable Flemish tapestries and perhaps the *tapissieries d'Auvergne,* also known more famously as Aubusson tapestries.[24] Whether the Bergamo or more treasured ones, tapestries were valuable possessions because of the labor, materials, and scale of production.[25]

Though essential to luxurious décor, none of these goods was uniquely French. Ultimately, it was in the realm of furniture design that the French found a decorative medium to express their national capacity for innovation, fashion, and splendor. This would be France's most important contribution to the interior, the design and production of distinctive and fashionable furniture. As its design departed from that of Italy and embarked on its own stylistic course, French furniture was acknowledged internationally for its unique qualities. Much of this innovation in design was sponsored by the crown, a process described in detail by Auslander; therefore, we label the major periods in French design in correspondence with the ruling monarch.

The style of Louis XIII is considered a transitional period during which French furniture makers began to depart from the design principles of the

Italian Renaissance and to forge something new. Louis XIII furniture was reminiscent of the sixteenth century, and it did not proclaim French ingenuity in the way the furniture of the late seventeenth century would. Some have gone so far as to argue that during this reign the "furnishing arts did not display any strongly marked national character either in France or elsewhere."[26] Still, most agree it was a beginning, and Louis XIII furniture was commonplace in Dauphiné.

The basic features of Louis XIII furniture were heavily geometric, described as austere by one historian. The furniture was simple in concept and purpose; it consisted of chairs, tables, beds, chests, armoires, and desks. Adornment was presented in relief carving, much of which was also geometric, and in the use of turning. Turning was the most important feature of decoration, and it clearly defined this period in French furniture history. Artisans turned chair legs, table legs, table stretchers, chests, and the *colonnettes* (engaged columns) on armoires. The most common form was the spiral leg, and furniture makers used as well the baluster leg and the leg *en chapelet* (also known as the rosary or knob leg). They fashioned furniture from common woods such as oak, walnut, pearwood, and pine, with exotic materials such as ebony, ivory, marble, and stone used to inlay decorative details (fig. 2.1).[27]

In dramatic contrast to the previous period, furniture during the reign of Louis XIV was less geometric and much more ornamental. The longest reign in European history saw furniture design pass through distinct phases, but some defining and overarching characteristics can be isolated. Louis XIV furniture remained reliant on straight lines, though these were often softened by the decorative overlay of curved lines and ornamentation. Materials were varied and exotic, and furniture makers employed marquetry more as decoration. Finishes included a French effort to imitate Chinese lacquer (*vernis façon Chine*), and French consumers showed a preference for furniture gilded in gold. Furniture legs were completely different from those of the previous era; common were both the square baluster leg and the curved console leg with hooved foot. Furniture types introduced included commodes, console tables with matching gueridons, buffets, and writing tables. Seating became more elaborate, and the day bed, though of earlier appearance, is most closely associated with this reign. Sofas or

FIGURE 2.1. LOUIS XIII–STYLE CHAIR AND CABINET

All illustrations by Teresa Rodriguez

the *canapé* expanded seating options, and the types of chairs evolved, a subject addressed in a later chapter. As finishing elements, bronze handles and mountings finished in gold, a technique known later as ormolu, were introduced in the period (figs. 2.2 and 2.3).[28]

Beyond mere style, certain pieces of furniture (the cabinet is a good example) directly projected the wealth and taste of a family. Prior to the seventeenth century cabinets were small and portable; now the cabinet emerged as a substantial piece, and the most precious examples were highly ornamental. Near the end of the 1600s, wealthy families expressed a decided preference for cabinets ornamented in an exotic manner, to include decoration mimicking Chinese or Japanese varnishes. Often cabinetmakers finished their work with black lacquer and gold gilt; sometimes they trimmed cabinets in tortoiseshell, bronze, or brass. Cardinal Mazarin owned a cabinet that was fashioned in the shape of a pagoda. Cabinets could be objects of splendor, and they might contain treasured objects and collections.[29] *Ébénistes* produced elaborately decorated furniture, usually tables, cabinets, or wardrobes. They typically focused on surface decoration, and often their furniture was veneered, inlaid, and accented with gilded bronze (ormolu) fixtures.[30]

Beds, through designs and by the textiles that bedecked them, offered other striking pieces of furniture on display, and because the *chambre* in which one slept was also a public space, it too was on display. Good reason, then, for elaborate curtains and hangings to create a more private space within for the bed. A bed was "not only an object for comfort, as we consider it today, but a source of prestige, endowed with a symbolic and sentimental value."[31] The importance of one's bed, symbolic or otherwise, is revealed by the fact that the first item described in an inventory was usually the bed occupied by the deceased. Notaries described beds in greater detail than any other items within a household, and Pardailhé-Galabrun finds that in Paris beds were so important that their value was often disproportionate to the wealth of the family.[32]

On display commonly were four-poster beds furnished elaborately with draperies, canopy, and coverlets. They mostly consisted of posters, a tester or flat roof, and an elaborate series of draperies that created an enclosed space. Often finials rested on top of the four posters, adding a decoration

FIGURE 2.2. LOUIS XIV–STYLE CONSOLE

FIGURE 2.3. LOUIS XIV–STYLE CABINET WITH
MARQUETRY DESIGNS

to an otherwise simple roofline. This bed type was popular throughout Europe during the period 1620–80 and was known as the *lit en housse* (also *lit à housse*) or, more commonly, the "French bed." As described, beds of this type appear in a number of Abraham Bosse's engravings (fig. 2.4). In most cases only little wood showed; it was the accompanying textile furnishings that transformed the bed into an object of magnificence.[33] These might include curtains, usually four, that hung from rings on iron rods; *cantonnières* and *bonnegrâces,* or narrow curtains that closed the corner gaps; and valances (*pentes*), both inner and outer (outer valances often decorated with trim). In addition, counterpane (or *contre point*) served as a sort of bedspread. It covered the bed and fit around the posts, and it included three panels that fell down the sides of the bed. Its design was geometric and meant to lie flat with squared edges. Finally, finials rested above the tester on the four posts. With draperies closed, the bed maintained a square, boxlike shape. The basic elements and form of the *lit en housse* were established in the reign of Louis XIII, and the outfit is described in this way:

> The wooden framework is of comparatively little importance, after the correct proportions have been assured. The *ciel,* or canopy, which is supported by four posts must never quite touch the ceiling of the room. The posts are covered with the same material as the curtains, or painted in harmony, and occasionally they are left plain. Iron rods surround the canopy beneath the valance for the support of the curtains, which may be drawn up or down by means of cords and pullies. When closed, the *lit en housse* has the appearance of a square box. The *lit en housse* consists therefore of the four posts, the canopy or *ciel,* the headboard and the base around which the lower valance is fastened. The canopy is always lined and surrounded by a valance, which is repeated around the base. The straight curtains that hang from the canopy in rigid lines behind the headboard (or bolster if there is no headboard) are known as *bonnegrâces.* From the canopy and underneath the valance hang the three outside curtains. The counterpane, called *courtepointe,* or *couverture de parade,* is generally of the same material as the curtains or their linings. The bolster is always long and round. Pillows never occur.[34]

Later in the century the *lit imperiale* and the *lit à duchesse* emerged as stylish alternatives to the boxy "French bed." Their major structural difference was the tester, which was now suspended from the ceiling by the use of cords. The *lit à duchesse* offered a variation on this theme with a half

FIGURE 2.4. A *LIT EN HOUSSE*

tester above and curtains pulled back instead of hanging straight. Near the end of his reign Louis XIV is supposed to have slept at least some nights in a *lit à duchesse* (fig. 2.5).[35]

The textiles used for bed hangings included tapestry, brocade, damask, silk, velvet, serge, and linen. Beds were also outfitted with calicoes or *indiennes,* which could be either Indian imports or European facsimiles. Notaries described the trimmings on curtains and counterpanes; a magnificently furnished bed would be trimmed in fringe, galoons, braids, laces, or tassels. Braids could be woven of gold or silver threads for a particularly opulent effect. And, in the case of the *lit en housse,* the final touches were often a finial atop each of the four corners consisting of plumes or carved wooden knobs.[36]

Notaries paid much attention to the furnishings for the bed, commencing with the condition and quality of the mattress. Mattresses could be stuffed with wool, straw, or horsehair. They were covered with white linen sheets, and the top sheet was usually decorated along the top edge, which would display when turned down. Sheets were then covered by a number of woolen blankets, covered in turn by one or more quilts. Finally, this virtual mound would be topped off with a *contre point,* or counterpane, matched or coordinated with the bed hangings. The occupant might then rest his or her head on a bolster filled with feathers.[37]

Lastly, the fashionably appointed residence included clocks. While their mechanical and utilitarian qualities most profoundly affected European society, it was their aesthetics that rested uppermost in a family's decision to acquire clocks. They were objects of splendor, and Parisian clockmakers turned out exquisite examples of pendulum clocks. Indeed, the great *ébénistes* of France constructed the cabinetry for the most coveted case clocks.[38] Expense and availability limited access, and many elite families did not own one. In the reign of Louis XIV the pendulum clock, encased in a marquetry or gilded case, was an exceptional luxury (fig. 2.6).[39]

Ownership of these most important goods defined luxury. So what households served as the archetypes that inspired provincial elites? What homes inspired elites in the provinces when they heard about, read about, or even saw these homes in person? The Hôtel de Rambouillet was one such trendsetting location, and we will address its importance later. But

FIGURE 2.5. A *LIT IMPERIALE* AND A *LIT DUCHESSE*

FIGURE 2.6. CLOCK BY BALTAZAR MARTINOT

other residences in Paris stood as templates for splendor. Among them was the Hôtel de Guise, formerly the Hôtel de Clisson, rebuilt and better known in the eighteenth century as the Hôtel de Soubise. Inventories of the *hôtel* conducted in 1644 and 1688 serve as testimony to the interior's evolution over the century. The 1644 inventory makes clear that the family regarded its collection of textiles and silver as its most precious possessions. The Guise had accumulated an extensive assortment of the finest tapestries available, including many examples identified by their points of origin—Flanders, Brussels, Auvergne (Aubusson), Paris, and Amiens. The family also owned a number of rugs, most from Turkey and one labeled Persian. And finally, their collection of textiles included elaborate and highly decorative furnishings and hangings for the so-called French beds.[40] This was seventeenth-century decoration on a grand scale, especially in the elaborate use of textiles, all supported by a growing collection of paintings (no reference to sculpture), many of which were portraits of family members painted by unnamed artists. The family also owned an extensive assortment of silver.

Forty years later the inventory of the household of the Duchess of Guise recorded some important additions and changes. For whatever reason, hers was a substantially shorter inventory. Perhaps significant items had been dispersed to other heirs since 1644 or by Mademoiselle herself, but there were meaningful changes in the contents of the Guise household. Most notable, the collection of paintings was given a higher status, as the attribution of artist appears regularly. The summit of this collection was a *Virgin* by Raphael and a *St. Catherine* by Da Vinci. She also owned a painting by Paul Veronese and works by Mignard, Teniers, and Juste D'Egmont, to name some of the more notable artists. Second, the great tapestries that adorned the *hôtel* in 1644 were no longer listed and had been replaced by a more modest collection. The growth of a substantial gallery of paintings and the relative decline of the tapestry in this one household may be evidence of a larger trend that climaxed in the 1700s and presaged the virtual disappearance of the wall hanging. The duchess's silver collection was also more modest than before, but crystal items compensated for any loss of brilliance. Her collection of crystal chandeliers was extensive, distributed throughout the *hôtel*, and valued at 6,321 livres.[41]

Furniture was seriously underrepresented in the 1688 inventory; yet we can form an impression of its grandeur and style by the few remaining pieces. Beds were furnished extravagantly, including one draped in crimson velour, trimmed with gold and silver *passementerie,* and lined with crimson satin and gold and silver borders. Tables and cabinets were of marquetry and embellished with materials including tortoiseshell and ivory. An assortment of nearly one hundred orange trees and their boxes breathed life and exoticism into both grounds and *hôtel.* Her estate also included seventy-four containers of Spanish jasmine, two large pomegranate trees, and forty large bay laurel trees in boxes.[42]

The Guise household was just one that may have inspired provincial consumers, and there were many others. In 1698 Dr. Martin Lister, a naturalist and physician, accompanied the Earl of Portland on a diplomatic mission to France, one result of which was a travel account of his observations. Earlier in life Lister had studied at the University of Montpellier, and it is clear that this Englishman was a seventeenth-century Francophile. He recalled with amazement much of what he saw and experienced on this trip, not the least of which was the splendor of Parisian aristocratic homes. Francophile though he might have been, it is also clear that Lister did not approve of the profligate ways of the French aristocracy:

> As the Houses are Magnificent without, so the Finishing within side and Furniture answer in Richness and neatness: as Hangings of rich Tapestry, raised with Gold and Silver Threads, Crimson Damask and Velvet Beds, or of Gold and Silver Tissue. *Cabinets* and *Bureau's* of Ivory inlaid with Tortoisshell, and Gold and Silver Plates, in a hundred different manners: Branches and Candlesticks of Crystal: but above all, most rare Pictures. The Gildings, Carvings and Paintings of the Roofs are admirable.
>
> These things are in this City and the Country above, to such a variety and excess, that you can come into no private House of any Man of Substance, but you see something of them; and they are observed frequently to ruine themselves in these Expenses. Every one that has any thing to spare, covets to have some good Picture or Sculpture of the best Artist: The like in the Ornaments of their Gardens, so that it is incredible what pleasure that vast quantity of fine things give the curious stranger. Here as soon as ever a Man gets any thing by Fortune or Inheritance, he lays it out in some way as now named.[43]

Not all Englishmen were as sympathetic to the French and their material culture as Dr. Lister, and, in fact, many wrote with a critical amusement about them. Almost a century later John Andrews, describing their vanity and their possessions, claimed that "no people so much delight in regaling their audience with an endless catalogue of their domestics, equipages, horses, houses, furniture, and every other appurtenance of that nature." Andrews grudgingly admitted that, even when bragging about their property, the French managed to introduce the subject "with so much art as not to seem out of place; and [the topics] are sometimes managed with so much dexterity as even to afford amusement."[44]

Descriptions of these residences reached Dauphiné and the periphery through design publications and by firsthand accounts like that of Lister. Publications by architects and designers went well beyond simply describing an interior; some offered detailed plans for interior decoration. Families could furnish their homes according to descriptions clearly inspired by Paris and Versailles; this explains why elite homes in Dauphiné were remarkably the same as their counterparts in Guyenne and conformed to a clearly defined elite style that was both French in origin and international in reach.

The household of Joseph de Mérindol, Sieur de Vaux and Treasurer for the Wars in Dauphiné, presents a relatively early example of how splendor was interpreted in the provinces. Mérindol descended from a cadet branch of an old Provençal noble family that had established in Dauphiné in the late sixteenth century. His was only the third generation to reside there.[45] In fact, the family established in Dauphiné precisely as the *procès* was reaching fevered pitch. Issues of actual antiquity aside, we can speculate that the family's reception in the community was similar to that of *anoblis*. It was surely perceived as part of the problem, that is, just one more family whose territorial acquisitions added to the burden of the Third Estate.

The inventory of Mérindol's household took place in 1680–81, and it revealed the family's purchasing power and interest in art. The contents of this household are discussed in several chapters, but here we consider some of its main luxurious design elements, among them an extensive collection of paintings. In fact, the Mérindol collection is distinguished by the number of secular subjects it contains:

—a portrait of the king (no king specified)
—a painting of a woman crying
—six landscapes
—a seascape
—four paintings, each representing one of the seasons
—one painting of a deceased woman surrounded by three other people
—three still-lifes of flowers
—three still-lifes of fruit[46]

Beyond his collection of paintings, Mérindol's outstanding possessions included a cabinet in the style of Louis XIII (with legs twisted) with marquetry details in ivory. Other furnishings resembled this piece, among them a Louis XIII table trimmed with ivory and matching chairs. For the most part, his furniture, though ample, appears to derive from the earlier part of the century. Still, there were pieces more recently made and more representative of trends in the 1680s. For example, a small table transitional in its design straddled the periods of Louis XIII and Louis XIV, with legs that were twisted columns and finished with a Chinese style varnish and trimmed in gold.[47]

The single most impressive inventory cataloged the possessions of Gabriel Aymon de Franquières, a judge in the Parlement of Grenoble. There is some question about the exact date of his family's ennoblement (1593 or 1603), but it is clear that this family was among the *anoblis* who bore the brunt of the Third Estate's legal assault.[48] Reasons for its ennoblement are subject to debate; some sources indicate that military service provided entry into the Second Estate, while others suggest that it was for the family's work in the Parlement. Its sixteenth-century history offers evidence of the ease with which families in this province moved between the realms of sword and robe. By the late seventeenth century, the eldest sons in the family pursued careers in the Parlement, and the younger sons sought careers in military service.[49]

Gabriel and his wife, Marie de Beauxhostes d'Agel, the daughter of a president of the Chambre des Comptes in Montpellier, had a home in Grenoble and a château in the countryside. The contents of both were not only ample but on trend, and they offer evidence of the evolution of interiors from the time of Mérindol's death in 1680 to that of the judge in 1717.[50] In Gabriel's country home there were many fashionable and expensive goods, including marquetry furniture and a case clock signed by Baltazard Martinot. This clockmaker designed for the king himself, and his clocks were considered some of the period's best.[51] But, while impressive, the country house was surpassed by the interior of Gabriel's urban residence. His *hôtel* housed an enormous collection of silver, to be discussed later, and many of its furnishings reflected the styles of the late seventeenth century, particularly the increased use of gold gilding. Much of Franquière's furniture was gilded. Gone are references to twisted columns; routine now are the marquetry details. Beds were elaborate as always, but in both residences this family made a design statement by the use of the very fashionable *lit à duchesse*. Also striking is the virtual disappearance of the tapestry, now replaced by paintings

The location of these possessions tells us how the lifestyle of the Franquières varied from town to country. In town their goods were on display. The urban townhouse was the scene of both frequent entertaining and work; people, other *parlementaires* and the urban community in general, came and went routinely. Preparation for the courtroom took place there, which explains the great collection of law books and the number of desks and secretaries. At its rural residence the family entertained less, enjoyed more leisure, and lived in a manner that was more relaxed and perhaps more traditional for nobility. But this is not to suggest that the rural residence was without spectators. Certainly, the Franquières entertained there as well, and maybe entertained the local community in the traditional spirit of aristocratic hospitality, but their routines and daily activities were quite different in the countryside.

How exactly were these differences reflected in the material goods of each residence? The urban interior was distinguished by a consistent use of mirrors, gold, stylish furniture, and paintings. Consider the contents of a single room where the use of gold and mirrors alone must have resulted in a spectacular effect. The room included an Imperial-style bed outfitted with a canopy, drapes, and skirts in *point d'Angleterre* tapestry, embellished with silk fringe and lined with red toile. Seating consisted of fifteen high-backed chairs decorated with gilded flowers and upholstered in tapestry to match the bed. Other pieces of furniture included a Louis XIV–style ormolu-mounted, nine-drawer cabinet, trimmed with tortoiseshell marquetry. In addition, there were two gold gilded tables with matching pairs of gueridons. The family appointed the room with two mirrors each styled with pediments of glass, perhaps from Venice, and a third mirror with a gilded frame. Here was also displayed a case clock with marquetry details signed by the Parisian clockmaker Claude Duchesne. Finally, positioned above the fireplace was a particularly large (eighteen-piece) ceramic *garniture de cheminée* that by virtue of its size must have caught the eye of anyone who entered.[52]

This different use of urban and rural spaces seems to have been commonplace among local elites. For the family of Jean de Vincent there was clearly an important distinction between urban and rural residences. Vincent, who was *conseiller tresorier* to the *generalité* of Dauphiné, died in 1691 and left behind a large estate that included a *hôtel* in Grenoble and a château in the countryside.[53] His noble background is unclear, but it is reasonable to assume that the family was among those most recently ennobled. Some sources report that a previous Jean Vincent, also *tresorier,* was ennobled in 1653.[54] It appears certain that he was the father of our Jean de Vincent. Sources also maintain that the elder Jean was the son of Pierre de Vincent, an attorney in the Parlement who purchased a seigniorie in 1625, for which he did homage a few months later.[55] These conflicting reports aside, the family's association with the *generalité* and matters of tax collection strongly suggests that it had been ennobled only recently. The inventory of Vincent makes the difference between urban and rural residence particularly striking. In town were the most costly and fashionable goods, and in town was located his impressive collection of tapestries, which included a six-piece tapestry from Flanders and a nine-piece Aubusson set. Here the family hung its three cartouches above interior doors. The cartouche became a fashionable decorative element during the seventeenth century, and by the eighteenth century cartouches appeared commonly in aristocratic homes. By their design they offered another opportunity for a family to celebrate its antiquity and lineage. They often appeared as broken scrolls with ovals or open spaces in the center where the family could display its armorials or an inscription.[56]

Although there is evidence that the family of François-Alexandre de Perissol-Alleman owned an apartment in Grenoble, only an inventory for their château at Allières conducted in 1708 remains in existence. This was a family of *anoblis* whose nobility dated only from 1604 and was due to the accomplishments of Samson de Perissol, a judge in the Chambre de l'Edit from 1601 made president in 1622. He pursued a strategic marriage to Blanche Alleman, whose father was the Seigneur d'Allières. She was an only child, and at her father's death his entire vast estate passed into the Perrisol line. François-Alexandre was the grandson of this union and ultimately heir to the office of president to the Chambre de l'Edit.[57]

The inventory lists a predictable array of goods as its most salient feature, but the household stands out by virtue of its *orangerie* and collection of fifty-two orange trees, some large and some small. According to the notary, the trees had suffered mightily in the past winter and presumably from neglect (perhaps as a result of the death of the seigneur). They were not standing in the *orangerie* but rather in the *parterre*. They are described in detail down to their dried leaves and broken branches. The orange trees were mostly contained in traditional wooden boxes painted white and blue, and the botanical collection was enhanced by a large assortment of other plants, including jasmine and fig trees that had suffered the same dismal fate. By his careful attention to detail and by his narrative description, walking us through the *parterre*, it is clear that for this notary the exotic garden was just that—an exotic form of luxury goods. What may have served as the seigneur's gardening inspiration was the copy of *Le Mercure galant* that appeared in his library.[58] Moreover, he was not the only nobleman in the region to own a collection of orange trees; the Franquières had also acquired a similarly impressive collection.

Few noble families had the financial capacity to decorate on the scale of the Franquières or the Vincents. Fiscal and decorative limitations, however, were always relative, and provincial elites generally included a plentitude of *parlementaire* households whose resources were more modest but still distinguished them in the eyes of the larger urban community. These households did not have multiple residences and extensive landed investments, and their ability to consume, while impressive in a local context, seemed modest compared with the families that truly towered over all others financially. Still, their inventories are in some ways the most revealing. When purchasing power is limited, the choice of objects takes on even greater importance. The furnishings of these households were often eclectic in style; they owned more furniture from the earlier period; and yet often they superimposed on a rather traditional and dated interior certain key goods that resonated with current fashion and luxury. An ideal example of this selective effort to update can be seen in the house in Grenoble that belonged to Pierre Duchon, a judge in the Chambre des Comptes. The origins of Duchon's family are obscure but clearly *anoblis.* There are references to an ancestor, Pierre Duchon, who was *procureur* for the *bailliage* in 1612,[59] but this position would not have conferred nobility. At some point later in the century the family was ennobled, apparently for service in the Chambre des Comptes. Its presence in the court is documented to 1628 when a Duchon served as *maître* in the Comptes.[60] At the end of the century our Pierre was both *conseiller* and *maître* in the Comptes; he is referred to occasionally as *noble;* and he married the Madeleine de Vivier, a widow who brought to the union the seigniorie of Rochechinard.[61] It is possible that he was the first in his family to enjoy noble status.

The year of the Duchon inventory was 1719, and, in an otherwise unremarkable house outfitted in a manner more appropriate for 1680, there were a handful of very trendy and striking accessories. Among them was a large *garniture de cheminée* that consisted of seventeen pieces of faience. In the next room, the notary logged a mirror with frame and pediment also constructed of a mirror, a style representative of Louis XIV. Above the fireplace, positioned to great advantage, was a trumeau framed in gold, and in an adjacent room hung a mirror with ormolu details. Duchon also owned an extensive collection of silver bearing his family arms.[62] By the addition of these brilliant items, the Duchon residence was instantly given a facelift.

The Grenoble home of Antoine Drogat (also inventoried in 1719), an attorney in the Parlement, was furnished similarly. In describing the furniture the notary noted the spiraled legs of the dated Louis XIII style. But one room stands out in this otherwise entirely predictable inventory. It was outfitted with a sofa, a *garniture de cheminée* composed of nine porcelain objects and two plaster representations of dogs, and a collection of paintings, mostly landscapes. A pair of brass sconces flanked the fireplace.[63] By concentrating its most fashionable goods in a single room, this family had clearly positioned them for their greatest impact. It is particularly noteworthy that the Drogat family appears to have suffered the unfortunate effects of the fateful settlement of 1602. A member of the family is listed among the *avocats consistoriaux* whose noble status was reduced in 1602 to *personnelle;* he remained noble, but his family was not ennobled in perpetuity.[64] Drogat's family, claiming nobility, essentially lost it, at least temporarily, as a result of the *procès.* Concomitantly, Pierre Duchon was from a family that acquired nobility much later and during the great battle over taxation and social status lived as part of the prosperous Third Estate. The family's convergent consumer choices at the end of the century may well have been influenced by its social disappointments and setbacks at the beginning of the century.

What we can discern in these inventories is that elite families in Dauphiné assiduously acquired goods that allowed them to present a particular and carefully constructed image. Some families had the means to do this in a particularly grand, consistent, and wholesale manner; others could achieve the effect of style and luxury only by the acquisition of fewer carefully chosen and strategically placed objects. In both groups the impulse to acquire and to do so in a way that reflected the fashionable trends of Paris is clear. As consumers, this provincial elite participated in a rapidly emerging national culture of the decorative arts and in a broader international culture of splendor and luxury.

REGULARITÉ
COLOR SCHEMES AND MATCHED SETS

O ne hallmark of the French style of interior decoration was the concept of *regularité,* the harmonious, unified effect found in a room, indeed within a residence, and achieved by a deliberate use of color and matched sets of furnishings. By the eighteenth century, this philosophy directed interior decoration in Paris and the provinces to the extent that rooms were painted and their furnishings upholstered in a single color and a single fabric, embellished often with gold. The effort to create harmony and unity through color and reiteration of design and textiles began in the seventeenth century and by the eighteenth century was convention. Such uniformity and repetition had not always existed in French interiors but attained a popularity that would not be limited to France. The concept of *regularité* served philosophically more than any other trait to define a French national style to domestic and international elite audiences. Certainly, this included many critics and detractors, who responded negatively to its formulaic character,[1] but the audience also included an international population of moneyed elements whose homes became a place in which to showcase their taste and fluency in the French mode.

The French style before Versailles was largely defined by the Marquise de Rambouillet. Thornton attributes tremendous influence to the interior that the marquise very carefully constructed at her *hôtel.* The remodeling of Hôtel de Rambouillet began in 1619, and the marquise took an active part in its design. The principles that guided her choices included efforts to create a unified, harmonious effect, equivalent to one of the central goals of Italian architects during the Renaissance. By the early seventeenth century Italian design principles had gained sway in France and elsewhere in Europe. Having spent her youth in Italy, the marquise was clearly influenced by Italian designs and arrangements of interior spaces. To achieve the kind of harmony and unity she sought, extensive use was made of a single color or color scheme or single textile. Best known was the famous *Chambre bleue,* where she hosted salons. This setting was distinguished by its uniformity of color—the walls were painted blue and covered in blue fabric, and the chair covers and other textiles were in the same shade of blue. The use of such color schemes became closely associated with French design, and it apparently distinguished Rambouillet's interiors in the eyes of her guests, including Marie de Medici. Contemporaries commented admiringly about the *regularité* of the interior of her *hôtel,* an attribute that came to mark French style.[2]

An awareness of the decorative possibilities and effects of color helped to define interiors of the seventeenth century. Designs now made a much more consistent use of color and color schemes, and designers began to introduce new colors to the decorative palette. Over the course of the century unfolded an increasing reliance on color as a primary decorative feature. What came before Rambouillet was darker, more somber, and anything but studied in its use of color. Walls were covered in tapestries or leather hangings and furnishings upholstered in somber shades of red and brown. "The general impression had to be one of intimacy but also austerity." In striving for greater harmony and unity, what the marquise achieved at Rambouillet was to produce an interior that was light, airy, and more lively than what had come before.[3]

If Rambouillet set in motion the beginning of a revolution in style, as many have argued, Simon Vouet was a revolutionary whose ideas inspired additional change. The painter's return to France from Italy in 1627 marked the beginning of the decorative style in which color played a primary role. Alain Mérot argues for Vouet's importance and stresses the formative role of the years he spent in Italy. Vouet and his disciples preached the use of colors that were lighter, yet strong and even brilliant. His work popularized gold accents and the sort of nuanced palette associated with French design. This is not to suggest that suddenly all French interior decoration shifted to his preferred lighter palettes. Actually, Mérot maintains that at midcentury there was a resurgence of stronger colors, which he attributes to the tastes of "nouveaux riches" who desired a more spectacular effect.[4] And it is certainly the case that for the remainder of the century red (often in combination with green) remained the most commonly used color. But Vouet had precociously urged the paradigm shift that was realized later under Louis XIV.

By the late seventeenth century, the ideas of Vouet and others were widely practiced throughout France. The inventories make clear the popularity of color schemes and the reliance on color as a central feature of interior decoration. In their choice of vocabulary to describe color, the notaries revealed a growing consciousness of it and its coordinated use. They frequently ventured beyond the blunt instruments of primary and secondary colors to depict in significantly more discerning terms the different hues they observed in the interiors of these homes. They scrupulously noted colors such as *muse* (a brownish gray), *aurore* (the color of dawn, a yellow with light red tones, according to Lowengard), *feuillemorte* (a color that was based on green and reddish brown and gained popularity at the end of the sixteenth century), *citron* (a pale, lemon yellow that was used in the infamous home of Nicolas Fouquet), and *minime* (a somber shade of gray, taking its name from the religious order). *Incarnat* or *incarnadin* described a very vivid and pinkish red, one that supposedly approximated the color of freshly butchered meat. The notaries also differentiated among reds to include *feu*, the color of fire, *cramoisy*, crimson, or *ponceau*, another particularly lively red. *Isabelle* was an ivory or off-white derived from white and yellow. According to Henri Havard, it took its name from Isabella of Castille, who allegedly vowed at the siege of Granada not to change her white linens until the Spanish had succeeded.[5] Such dingy origins must have inspired only dimly the dyers who tinted fabrics in this creamy hue. (I should also note that modern uses of the term refer to a deeper brownish color.) What is most revealing about the use of *Isabelle* and these other names is the notaries' concerns for precise descriptions and nomenclature. In 1715, one notary described the accoutrements for a bed as the color of coffee (trimmed in aurora).[6]

All this attention to terminology was necessitated by new discoveries in chemistry that led to a proliferation of dyes and choices and with it a greater cultural awareness of color. Sarah Lowengard, who studies the technology, science, and culture of color making in the eighteenth century, points out that color names varied not only with language but also according to region, producer, and methods of production. The use of names was both a subjective and a scientific matter, and one color might have several names or a single term might refer to a range of colors.[7] Nomenclature was a complex process based on requirements to convey systematically both quality and visual characteristics. Fashion, consumer trends, and marketing further complicated the process of naming. We know about some colors that a single name could mean several things, according to time and place, and that a color's meaning could evolve over time. According to Lowengard, aurora is a perfect example of how a color could change somewhat in meaning. In the seventeenth century and most of the eighteenth century it was yellow with light red tones. In the nineteenth century, it evolved into a yellowish light red.[8] Havard describes it as the latter, perhaps reflective of the fact that he produced his comprehensive work on furnishings in the nineteenth century.[9] Ultimately, the notaries' attention to color imparts information about the deliberative process by which acquisition took place. To achieve a decorative effect with color required more than planning and constancy; it required a vision of the end product and a very purposeful approach to acquisition.

As color and color schemes became a dominant feature of interiors, certain colors appear to have been especially fashionable. Under Louis XIV the most popular colors in Paris and the Bordeaux region were red and green, red being slightly more commonplace. This was also the case in Dauphiné. But red was not simply the primary red of the color wheel; as Pardailhé-Galabrun has noted, notaries listed variations that included crimson, cherry, vermilion, and scarlet. Later, in the eighteenth century, as tastes evolved along with the technology to produce new colors, consumers in Paris and Bordeaux tended to prefer more delicate colors and pastels.[10] In fact, she writes that "notaries used a vocabulary that was rich, precise and image-provoking all at once, thereby revealing the importance of these aspects of interior decoration."[11] Lowengard argues that color fashion changed quickly and observes that "owning and using fashionably coloured objects was a visual acknowledgement of participation in the social culture of the period."[12] She also notes that for a color to be good, and therefore popular, it had to be accepted as beautiful both as it stood alone and in combination with other colors. Pair composites worked only if each individual color remained as bright and lively as when each was used alone.[13]

Decoration by swathing a room and its furnishings in a single color (or pair of colors) and textile goes to the heart of a larger trend of achieving effect by seriality. Beyond the use of color, the matched set fundamentally defined French decorative style in this period. The serial use of textiles and furnishings created the unity and regularity that had become one of the cherished principles of French décor. Mimi Hellman has written persuasively to argue that seriality, a basic feature of the interiors of the period, was a form of consumption that was essential to elite self-fashioning. Repetition of color and textiles, matched sets of objects, and suites of paintings or garnitures were elements of seriality that acquired cultural and social significance. "The French interior was a space structured by sets, deliberately composed groups of objects in multiple media that played major roles in producing visual and spatial unity, regularity, emphasis, and animation."[14] The value of seriality, however, was associated not only with its visual impact. In an age before mechanized reproduction, the ability to recreate an object faithfully and painstakingly by hand was highly valued by the market and those who could afford to acquire these items.[15]

Textiles were a primary medium for both color and seriality, and matching suites of furniture and textile furnishings were therefore crucial in defining the French style. Textiles distinguished the homes of nobles to the extent that they became "the most conspicuous element of the décor of any house of importance."[16] These materials were expensive, and they were generally finished with intricate trimmings. Fabrics used on furniture also promoted the room's unified effect by virtue of their repetition. In fact, interior decoration was largely a matter of upholstery, which was much more elaborate than in previous periods. The same color and the same textile were used repeatedly throughout a room. Starting with the elaborate curtains and spreads on the bed, choices of fabrics created a dramatic focal point in the home's most important rooms.

Earlier I argued that beds were often the dominant element of a room's furnishings and objects of luxury. As such, they were outfitted with color-coordinated curtains or hangings, as well as coverlets. Chairs were covered with silk velvet and silk damask, or the less expensive option of woolen cloths such as velvet, and usually the colors of these fabrics matched or complemented the colors used in the bed according to a prescribed color scheme. Tapestry was also a possibility for chair covers and bed hangings, as was turkeywork, a woven fabric that resembled needlepoint and the patterns in Turkish rugs.[17] It was common to find the same textiles used to outfit both the bed and the chairs in a room. And families routinely possessed multiple sets of wall hangings and chair covers, which they changed according to season. During the period 1680–1730, chairs were commonly outfitted with slip covers that could be placed over the back and seats and then fastened in place with hooks and eyes. Many of these covers had deep skirts that changed the silhouette of the chair significantly.[18] Slip covers were options that enabled families to redecorate by simply changing colors and textures to accommodate climate and mood. As Thornton has noted, in order to redecorate, one simply had to call in an upholsterer.[19]

Serial upholstery of suites of furniture produced collections of matching items known as *meubles*. This could refer, for example, to an elaborately canopied bed complemented with fire screens, folding screens, armchairs, and side chairs. Or a *meuble* might consist of a sofa and chairs upholstered in the same fabric (fig. 3.1).[20] Furnishings proffered as a group and upholstered en suite became standard for formal spaces or any space in which the family received guests.[21]

Seriality as a theme also gave rise to a group of objects known as a garniture. A set of items made of the same material and decorated in the same manner, garniture embodied the design philosophy that found repetition and sameness aesthetically appealing. In the seventeenth century garnitures usually referred to a collection of objects used to decorate a fireplace.[22] *Garnitures de cheminée* were generally sets of three, five, or seven (or more) objects designed en suite to be used on mantles or on shelves above the mantles.[23] A typical garniture would include an assortment of vases, jars, cups, or figures, in faience or porcelain, of different but complementary shapes and sizes. The collection was then arranged, using formal

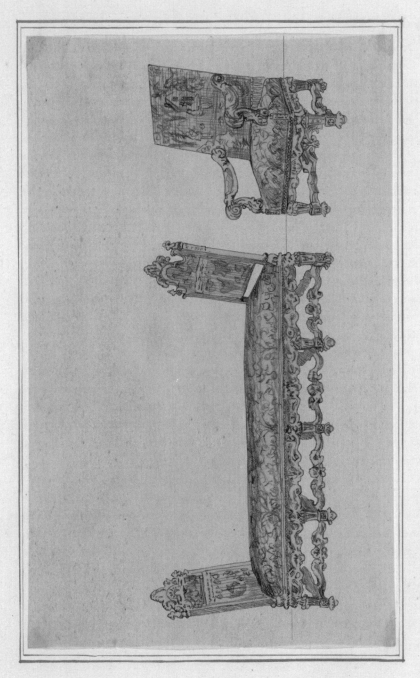

FIGURE 3.1. LOUIS XIV STYLE MEUBLE—DAYBED AND MATCHING CHAIR

FIGURE 3.2. A GARNITURE DE CHEMINÉE

symmetry, across the mantle of the fireplace. Or a large collection might be arranged on a variety of étagères hung above the mantle (fig. 3.2). In 1682 *Le Mercure* duly noted the appearance of such a garniture in the room dedicated to the goddess Diana at Versailles,[24] and publicity in *Le Mercure* was certain to guarantee popularity. Garnitures were not common in Dauphiné, but some did exist in the most affluent homes. The Franquières owned a large garniture of eighteen pieces of ceramic (the notary does not distinguish between faience and porcelain), which they used at their *hôtel* in Grenoble.[25] In 1719 two garnitures appear in the inventory of the more modestly furnished townhouse of Pierre Duchon, counselor to the Chambre des Comptes. The first consisted of eleven pieces, probably vases, and six *gobeaux,* or cups; the second set included four alabaster figures and two *gobeaux.*[26]

Reiteration of design was also at play in the creation of suites of tables and gueridons or candle stands. In the following chapter I discuss how candlestands promoted comfort and convenience, but here I want to emphasize that they were often carved and decorated to match or work in concert with a table. This meant that they bore the same marquetry or finish or that they were carved to resemble the pedestal of the table. To have a set of candle stands flanking and matching a table or commode, and perhaps a matching mirror hung over the table, would have made an important design statement (fig. 3.3). In Grenoble and environs suites of tables and gueridons were one of the most popular of all matched sets.[27]

Defined by color and repetition, the French style had radiated beyond the center to find its way to the frontier by the late seventeenth century. Among officeholders and the nobility in Dauphiné, this style of decoration had become standard. From one household to the other we find the same sorts of textiles and objects and, above all, the planned use of color. The major difference among households was one of scale and volume, as determined by wealth; the wealthier the family, the more likely it was to carry out a color scheme in detail and to have an alternative scheme in storage. Consistently, Dauphinois families projected color schemes in their important rooms, and sometimes they decorated several adjoining rooms in the same hues. The fact that textiles were often stored in trunks and armoires, sometimes in rooms other than those in which they were actually used,

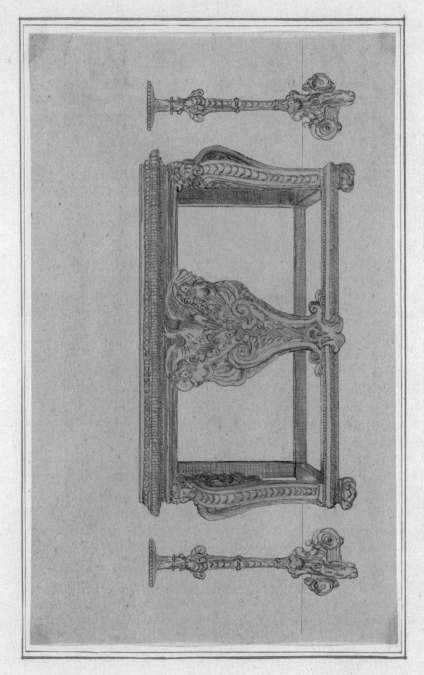

FIGURE 3.3. LOUIS XIV–STYLE CONSOLE AND MATCHING GUERIDONS

makes it difficult to situate the color scheme precisely, but we can form an impression of how color played out in the household.

The earliest inventory examined was conducted in 1668, when the heirs of Anne de la Croix, widow of Abel de Simiane La Coste, president of the Chambre des Comptes in Dauphiné and chevalier, commissioned a local notary to conduct an inventory of the contents of her household. Anne's father, Seigneur de Pisançon, was a noble of the sword whose career took him to Italy in the 1620s. Her mother was the daughter of a *parlementaire* family from Grenoble. The story of these two generations is typical for the region: sword meets and marries robe; robe moves easily and across generations between Parlement and the Chambre des Comptes.[28]

Starting with the room in which Anne died, the notary painstakingly recorded and described every item present. His list was comprehensive and detailed, and he was careful to mention the country of origin for imported items. He also took particular care to describe the color of the various textiles that had decorated the residence. Among the decorative elements were Flemish tapestries, Turkish rugs, coverlets from Catalonia and perhaps as far away as India. Her color scheme appears to have alternated, probably seasonally, between gray and red or crimson (embellished occasionally with gold) on the one hand and *feuillemorte* (embellished more consistently with gold) on the other.[29] The inventory leaves no doubt that the individual or individuals who decorated this home did so with a vision of color and the impact of its repetitive use. Both color schemes were typical of the mid-seventeenth century.

By 1708, the year a notary cataloged the estate of François-Alexandre de Perissol-Alleman, discussed earlier, color schemes had changed significantly. The main rooms of his château were systematically decorated in blue, yellow, and aurora. The alternative scheme was red, and it was found mostly in storage. In one *chambre,* there was a walnut bed (which appears from the notary's description to have been *à l'imperiale*) outfitted with drapes and fabrics in blue, yellow, and aurora; twelve chairs with slipcovers in blue and yellow velvet; an arm chair in yellow tapestry; and another chair in blue with fringe in gray and aurora. The walls of this room were covered with a seven-piece *tapisserie de Bergame,* and a rug from Anatolia was draped over a walnut table.[30] This was a family of status and means that could easily afford to upholster according to a prescribed scheme, to execute it down to such details as fringe, and to adhere to it throughout the prominent rooms of the château. In 1708, blue, yellow, and aurora would have appeared the more stylish alternative to the older red covers in storage. And how exactly did the family learn that current style was moving away from the reds of the *grand siècle* and toward blues and pastels? Again, a clue is in the single copy of the *Le Mercure galant* among François-Alexandre's books.

Pierre de Ponnat, Sieur de Merley, died in 1697 and left an estate that included an apartment in Grenoble as well as a château. His family had been ennobled in the sixteenth century and seems to have shifted easily between military and judicial careers in the Parlement. Ponnat himself followed a military path that earned him the title of lieutenant of the marshals of France, and he married the daughter of a military noble.[31] Ponnat and his wife maintained a home in Grenoble whose color scheme rotated seasonally, or by whim, among greens, blues, and the combination of yellow and violet. In a third-floor room the family stored an immense array of textiles and linens, few of which varied from these schemes. Tucked away in storage were an eleven-piece set of drapes and accoutrements for a bed in blue damask with silk fringe, twelve chair covers in the same blue damask, three green coverlets embroidered with the family's crest, a six-piece set of green drapes for a bed, a green table cover, a fourteen-piece set of drapes and accoutrements for a bed in yellow and violet, twelve coordinating needlepoint chair covers in yellow and violet, and twelve additional chair covers in yellow. The family chose to decorate its urban residence in the more fashionable colors of blue, violet, and yellow. The château, on the other hand, was furnished with textiles in more traditional seventeenth-century schemes of red and green, though here too were found a few items in yellow and violet.[32] To no surprise, the Ponnat family put its most fashionable foot forward in its most visible dwelling because the social impact of its acquisitions and style would have been significantly greater in an urban context.

Most other families showcased their more high-profile urban residence in preference over their country house. The townhouse and château of

Jean de Vincent are a perfect example. The former was particularly well appointed in shades of red, including crimson and *incarnat,* and in green. These colors were used not only consistently but in abundance, as the Vincent townhouse stood as a prime example of the "aesthetics of surplus." The draperies of one bed were executed in crimson, and twelve chairs had slipcovers to match. Although the notary failed to indicate the color of their upholstery, the family also owned a set of eighteen chairs *à chapelet* and two dozen chairs upholstered in velvet. And, should seating prove insufficient, this family could fall back on a set of twelve matching highbacked fauteuils upholstered in leather. Amazingly, these were not all the sets of chairs to be found in the townhouse. The number of matching sets of chairs made a dramatic statement, but so did other kinds of sets. For example, the Vincents owned a desk with matching gueridons.[33]

In contrast, Vincent's château was decorated in a less studied or consistent manner; indeed, the inventory of this rural residence suggests no real color scheme at all. The château housed an assortment of textiles and colors, but no single hue dominated. It was amply furnished, including forty chairs covered with leather accented with gold and four tables each with a matching set of gueridons. In general, however, its contents were less fine than those listed for his townhouse. Most notable, Vincent's collection of silver appears in the townhouse and not at the château.[34]

The Franquières decorated their urban residence predictably and consistently in reds and greens, and rarely did the family digress from these colors. Crimson, cherry, and green occur repeatedly throughout the inventories of both the urban and rural dwellings. Only occasionally did the notary mention yellow, violet, and blue. Perhaps the Franquières had just begun to introduce a different palette in their homes. As he registered the contents of an enormous chest, the notary found the following:

 —eighteen chair covers in crimson damask
 —a twenty-piece set of bed hangings in crimson with gold and silver trim
 —another set of bed hangings in crimson damask
 —a third, five-piece set of bed hangings in tapestry, with a background of
  citron and flowers in cerise
 —an assortment of other items made of tapestry in unspecified patterns and
  colors.[35]

For some families, décor was effected by the repetitive use of a single polychromatic textile, as in the case of the home of Abel de Charency. This modest robe family was ennobled in the late seventeenth century.[36] In decorating its home the family relied on the very popular tapestry weave known as *point d'Hongerie*. This chevron pattern appeared in two of the main rooms of the home. Distributed between the rooms were seven upholstered fauteuils and two chairs in point *d'Hongerie,* in addition to a *lit à duchesse* completely outfitted in the textile.[37] Given the bold geometric design of the multicolored chevron pattern, the effect must have been lively.

As pronounced as these design principles were in the homes of the wealthiest and most prominent families, the fact that families of more modest means implemented the same style divulges equally important information. The residence of Jean Baptiste Rigo, an ordinary attorney in Parlement, is an example of a household developed through greater expenditure than that made by most people belonging to a similar professional and social status. Rigo's family history is impossible to establish with any certainty, owing to variations in the spelling of his name. It appears that the family was ennobled in 1606 for military service and then purchased a seigneurie in 1624.[38] The home was furnished in an elaborate and entirely familiar manner: two Turkish rugs, four large *tapisseries de Bergame,* and thirty-two paintings (including several portraits). The real marker of wealth, the collection of silver, included flatware, serving pieces and candleholders. The inventory also indicated an effort to unify the interior by color and textiles. For instance, the family furnished one room with a large walnut bed (*à l'imperiale*) outfitted with draperies in *point d'Angleterre*. In the same room we find a dozen chairs upholstered in the same tapestry, two banquettes in the same tapestry, two smaller chairs in cross stitch, and a large fauteuil in *point d'Angleterre.* The room was also appointed with a Turkish rug, a six-piece wall tapestry in the popular foliage pattern, and coordinating *portières* in green damask. In addition to having upholstered most of the furnishings en suite, this family also furnished the room with a table and a desk each accompanied by a pair of matching gueridons.[39]

The 1719 inventory of the more modest household possessions of Antoine Drogat also reveals a consistent application of color. The room in which Drogat left this world was decorated in red and green. Its furnishings were all color coordinated and included eleven walnut chairs with high backs, one arm chair, six walnut chairs with short backs, a screen, two banquettes, one walnut table with a red leather cover, and a smaller walnut table with a green tablecloth, green draperies, and a six-piece set of Bergamo tapestries. By 1719 the red and green scheme was surely out of vogue, and one is struck by the consistency of its application. In another room the family adorned a fireplace with a garniture of nine pieces of porcelain flanked by two plaster figures of dogs.[40]

Imagine the home of Jean Amat, a simple *procureur* for the *bailliage*. The home was not large and not specially decorated, except for the principal room. In it there was a concerted effort to execute a sophisticated and subtle color scheme. The bed was outfitted in hangings in the color *minime* with silver trim. Poised at the four corners of the bed frame were four silver eagles. The gray theme was repeated on a table cover and on the upholstery of a dozen chairs. The room also included a *meuble* of six chaises *à la royale* and one fauteuil. On one wall hung a mirror with a walnut frame and ormolu mounts.[41] The Amat family, or so genealogists have maintained, descended from a very old Dauphinois family whose nobility dated from the fourteenth century. More likely is that a single branch dates from this period and that a number of other branches had to reestablish nobility by service. The family, in all its various branches, did survive the great *recherche* into nobility in 1667. It is interesting, however, that Jean Amat registered his family's armorial only in 1696, suggesting that his branch of the family had come by its nobility earlier in the seventeenth century.[42]

In the Grenoble home of another attorney, François Besset, we see again the repetitive use of color, in this case the much more stylish combination of pink and green. The main room of this smallish apartment in Grenoble housed a bed decked out in pink and green, four chairs with slipcovers in pink, two chairs with slipcovers in a floral satin with a green border, and a fauteuil with a slipcover in floral satin with a pink border. In addition there was a *canapé* in the room covered in pink and green taffeta. (According to Havard, *gros de tour* taffeta was especially popular in the late seventeenth and eighteenth centuries.[43]) Besset lived in an apartment, rather than a *hôtel*, and the inventory of his holdings is not especially lengthy. What is striking, however, is the very stylish nature of his possessions. He was on trend for

1714, if not ahead of his cohort. His color scheme anticipated the eighteenth-century preferences for pastels. His furnishings were upholstered in the satins, taffetas, and brocades that were so fashionable in the eighteenth century. In storage were older covers for his chairs in *point croisé*.[44] Perhaps they were put away to be pulled out in colder weather; perhaps they were old, out of style, and stored away indefinitely. What appears true is that Besset had recently redecorated in a very fashion-forward manner.

For many households it is clear that financial considerations precluded a unified approach to décor. Families of more modest resources were not in a position to execute a color scheme with any kind of consistency. And the colors that appear in their inventories are often past their fashion prime. *Feuillemorte,* for example, while still stylish in the 1680s, was out of fashion by the early 1700s. Yet among the less spectacular homes it still occurred. What appeared in these inventories was evidently a hodgepodge of older objects and items that the family could not afford to replace. These were not furnishings valued by virtue of age and patina. Undeniably, this was not an age or society that cherished patina in the way that later generations would. Antiquities, yes; antiques, no. When describing an object as old, the notary had in mind something that was not fashionable and that was not in good condition.

Without the repetitive use of textiles and colors, families were unable to achieve the same effect of seriality. This is not to say that these homes owned no sets; matching chairs can be found in all the homes inventoried. No home was without matching chairs upholstered or slip-covered in a single textile. The chair was the ubiquitous form of seriality. But it took a family of greater means to support repetition to the extent described by Hellman, and only the wealthier families owned the *meubles* and garnitures that were the hallmarks of French design.

What does this taste for repetitive design tell us about the society that purchased sets or decorated according to a color scheme? Sets were evidence of both wealth and taste. They cost more than singular items because the production of sets with reiterative forms was simply a more labor-intensive and therefore costly process. To reproduce by hand the same design over and over again was a laborious and painstaking process.[45] And by choosing sets over unmatched items, the consumer made an aesthetic as well as financial choice that placed him or her squarely within fashionable ranks. There was still more social significance to the choice of sets. Hellman argues that seriality served as a visual cue to guests who strived to perform and to project mastery of a code of polite conduct not easily negotiated. Upon entering a room, a guest could be guided toward appropriate conduct for the occasion by the furnishings. Series of matching chairs and furnishings arranged in rows along the walls indicated formality; mismatched chairs in smaller groups meant an evening of informal conversations. "Especially for a visitor to an unfamiliar space, the presence of such visual cues could make the difference between an elegant entry and an awkward one, and thus between the success or failure of social performance."[46]

The sheer volume of duplicated textiles and furnishings pointed to what Hellman calls the aesthetics of surplus. The fact that homes included more of a single item than could have been used at a single function, except on rare occasions, signified an effort to overwhelm the viewer with the weight of numbers. Hellman writes about a later period, but the aesthetics of surplus may apply, albeit in a more limited manner, to the late seventeenth century as well. In a later chapter I show that patterns of elite sociability were shifting to smaller formats and more intimate gatherings. No longer would there be the frequent need for twenty-five identical chairs in a single room. So what purpose did quantity continue to serve? Surplus and sets meant more than the power to consume in volume. The visitor was intended to be at once overwhelmed by the numerical power of this surplus and, by convention, was quite forbidden to stare at them, to handle them, or even to acknowledge them. Hellman points out that etiquette forbade this sort of behavior, so that, no matter how bedazzled the visitor, he or she had to resist the urge to express too much interest. Part of the social power of these objects was to set the visitor in "a position of unfulfilled desire."[47] The allure of repetition was foremost design unity and integration, but secondly, the power that it held over guests impressed by these objects of unrequited desire.

Finally, Hellman puts forth the suggestion that the acquisition of numerous matching goods served an inner psychological purpose, that repetition was a means of overcoming anxiety in circumstances of psychological uncertainty. She writes about the unstable world of elite society in eighteenth-century Paris, a world in which "social identities had to be constantly renegotiated." Recapitulation in this milieu brought a sense of order and conferred a sense of control or agency. The use of a single design over and over again reassured the owner and emphatically communicated social identity to the beholder. Dauphinois families lived in the unstable social world that flowed from the decades-long *procès des tailles;* here too the ownership of matching goods could serve soothingly as a psychosocial palliative. "In a world where the codes of decoration were inextricably bound up with those of social legitimacy, too much was never enough."[48]

The psychology of repetition aside, we know seriality was a central component of interior design and that it promoted the unified look that French consumers sought. The provincial families portrayed here subscribed to this design philosophy, and they used color, textiles, and matched sets to effect it. These decorative choices placed them in the larger community of elite consumers across France and assisted them in reconstructing an identity in a world that had earlier been rocked by their contumacious social inferiors.

COMMODITÉ
COMFORTS, CONVENIENCE, AND INNOVATION
IN FURNITURE AND LIGHTING

The relatively brief period 1680–1720 was crucial in the history of French household furnishings because it witnessed the growing popularity and wider distribution of furniture designed for comfort and convenience. This is the period in which consumers began to acquire furniture not just meant to be sat upon but actually designed to promote bodily comfort. This included design changes in chairs, accompanied by the rise of the sofa and the daybed, improvements in lighting, and the introduction of other conveniences. By the end of the seventeenth century there was a growing demand for furniture that allowed "a greater degree of repose."[1]

In France, the twin concepts of comfort and convenience were conflated by the term *commodité*, which was often attached to *chaise* or *fauteuil* to describe a particular type of easy chair that was in some ways the forerunner of the modern recliner. And by the turn of the century we find these items in homes not only in Paris, the epicenter of style, innovation, and furniture making, but also in more remote places like the frontier province of Dauphiné. Here innovative furnishings rapidly made their way into the households of noble families, suggesting a close relationship between cultural capital and imitative provinces. What was fashionable or state of the art in Paris soon gained sway over the imaginations and purses of provincial consumers as well. The growing presence of more comfortable furniture and conveniences pointed to changing ideas of luxury—not the abandonment of the exotic and opulent, but a broadening cultural notion that included what by modern standards would appear as rather practical. Comfort was a new form of luxury that elevated the importance of the body in design circles and redefined the relationship between luxury and necessity. Comfort was also closely associated with changes in architectural design to accommodate emerging notions of privacy and intimacy.

The idea that human physical comfort was a worthwhile goal was an early modern cultural construct. In the Middle Ages physical comfort was not a priority, and courtesy manuals addressed the issues of cleanliness and orderliness, but not the modern concept of comfort. John Crowley, who has written at length about the invention of the concept of comfort in the early modern period, points out that in the Middle Ages even the homes of people of means had very little furniture and seating.[2] It was in the early modern period and especially during the consumer revolution that house-hold goods proliferated, and by the late seventeenth and eighteenth centuries Europeans had turned more attention to furnishings designed for ease. Joan DeJean maintains that it was the French, specifically several notable French women, who inspired the modern home by embracing the design concept of comfort.[3]

How were ideas of comfort expressed in the period and what was meant by the terms *confort, le bien-être,* and *commodité*? The term *confort* retained its medieval sense and referred to a kind of moral quality of consolation until the mid-nineteenth century, when it assumed the more modern definition involving a physical state. It was the English who reconceptualized comfort, as they struggled with differences between luxury and necessity, to give it a physical emphasis. In the eighteenth century, however, physicality and the attendant emotional state of well being (*le bien-être*) were what the French meant when they attempted to express the abstraction later referred to as *confortable*.[4] By *commodité* the French referred to utility, ease, and convenience.[5] In talking about the rise of comfort, I am actually referring to *commodité,* and I have chosen to focus on items, that is, markers, that seem to be emblematic of this trend. Paramount among these is the chaise, or *fauteuil de commodité*.

What could suggest comfort more emphatically than a chair that was accommodating, deeply padded and upholstered, often with wings, and in some cases engineered so that the head could rest by lying back and the feet be elevated? The term *chaise* or *fauteuil de commodité* was applied to the easy chair certainly by 1680. The 1687 inventory of the furnishings of Louis XIV includes numerous references to chaises and *fauteuils de commodité* and to *fauteuil de commodité à cremaillière*.[6] This last appellation refers specifically to a chair with movable parts, with a design that incorporated a series of ratchets enabling the back to recline and the feet to rise—in this way, as John Crowley puts it, anticipating by almost three centuries the modern La-Z-Boy (not to mention ergonomics).[7] In fact, in his *Dictionnaire*, Furetière defined the simple *chaise de commodité* as a chair whose back could be lowered or raised by means of a *cremaillère* or rachet and on which one might sleep comfortably. In either case, movable parts or not, the design inspiration for these fauteuils was the comfort of the occupant as measured by the relationship between the chair and the body. Thornton argues that they likely evolved from chairs for the sick and from sleeping chairs. They gained popularity rapidly, but we know that they were not without critics. The presence of these chairs at court prompted concern over their effect on personal comportment. One courtier complained of the young men there by saying that if "there are large easy chairs, they commandeer them straightaway and are so uncivil as not to offer them to a lady; they stretch themselves upon them, they throw themselves back half lying down; they cradle themselves, they put their legs up on other seats or over one of the arms of the chair, they cross them and sometimes adopt postures that are even more indecent, believing that it lends an air of quality to use chairs in this way."[8]

For most, however, the *fauteuil de commodité* was not controversial; instead, it appears to have caught on rather quickly. Moreover, the term referred not only to chairs that were comfortable or easy but also to convenient models that included book stands or *pupitres* as well as writing tables. Utility composed another aspect of *commodité,* and it was for this purpose certainly that *pupitres* and small writing tables, with the capacity to swivel, were attached to these chairs. Furetière indicates in his dictionary that the term could apply to chairs equipped in this manner.[9]

The *lit de repos,* or daybed, also had become commonplace by the 1680s, and there is considerable evidence that it was popular much earlier in the century. We find them in Abraham Bosse engravings from the early seventeenth century. Later Madame de Maintenon had one in her bedchamber that was double ended, stood next to the wall, and included a canopy. The daybed was intended for resting, relaxing, reading, and informal conversation, and therefore it was considered a luxurious furnishing.[10]

The sofa (*sopha* or *saupha*) and the daybed share a common origin. They both appear to have evolved from a common ancestor, the *couche* or *couchette,* a simple bed, but the sofa did not emerge as a separate and distinct piece of furniture before the late seventeenth century. To contemporary minds, the term *sofa* reflected the Turkish inspiration for this new seating, known also as a *canapé.* There appears to have been no difference between sofa and *canapé,* and they became instantly popular in elite society. The Swedish ambassador wrote home in 1695 that "there is no room here without one" (fig. 4.1).[11]

Fauteuils, daybeds, and sofas were structured to promote relaxation and comfort. Suitable upholstery was also essential to complement this mission. Craftsmen used horsehair for the backs and for places that called for firmer padding. Down, on the other hand, was their choice for softness. According to Thornton, the *fauteuils de commodité* and sofas of the 1690s acquired their luxurious quality by the extensive use of down. He writes, in fact, that its use had become so widespread in Paris by the end of the century that contemporaries attributed a rising incidence of hemorrhoids to the fact that down had essentially replaced horsehair.[12]

These fashions in furniture spread rapidly to the provinces. At the same time that more comfortable furnishings were making their way into the homes of provincial elites, architects designed homes for them in ways that promoted greater privacy, models inspired, as always, by similar trends in Paris. Postmortem inventories reveal that increasing numbers of homes were designed to include more private and intimate spaces. And by the end of the century, French architects were addressing issues of privacy as they related to the arrangement of space. This became an essential feature of their work in the 1700s. By the late seventeenth century, rooms were for the most part multipurpose; bedrooms, or *chambres,* were public and

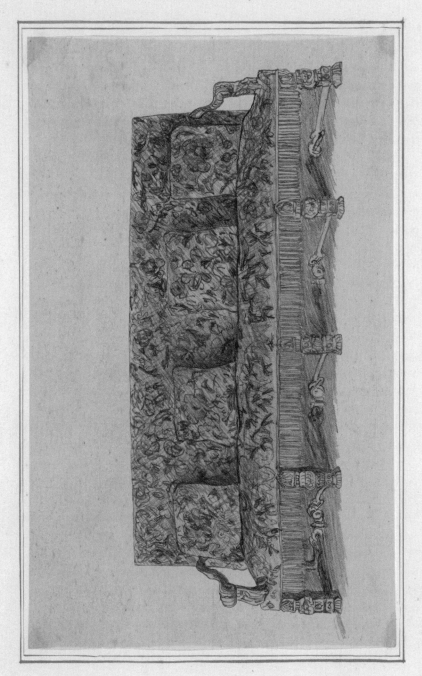

FIGURE 4.1. LOUIS XIV–STYLE SOFA

private space; they served both as sleeping quarters and as a place in which to receive guests. French design in the late seventeenth and eighteenth centuries was marked by the issue of spatial distribution and the effort to promote a more pleasant way of living. By pleasant is meant a new sensitivity to privacy facilitated by architectural incorporation of strictly private spaces. In 1710 Le Blond's revision of an earlier *Cours d'Architecture* postulated that the state rooms (*appartements de parade*) should appear in the front of the house and that private apartments (*appartements de commodité*) belonged in the rear.[13]

Institution of these new rules meant that by the eighteenth century most noble *hôtels* in Paris included three types of space—ceremonial, societal, and personal. The ceremonial rooms, or *appartements de parade,* were settings for displays of magnificence and hierarchy, for gatherings of individuals of unequal status. According to Katie Scott, these spaces were quite distinct from the *appartements de société,* which were instead devoted to gatherings of individuals of equal status. It was here that nobles hosted dinners, salons, and evenings of conversation and gaming.[14] *Cabinets* were small rooms often connected to bedchambers or apartments as a place of retreat and seclusion. These rooms "by their very nature were separate and were therefore freed from the conventions that governed the principal rooms."[15] And it was in *cabinets* that families tried out new forms of decoration and new forms of furniture, especially furniture designed for its commodious qualities. In Dauphiné the daybed was ubiquitous, the *chaise de commodité* and the sofa significantly less common but still recurring.

In the 1681 inventory of the estate of Joseph de Mérindol were two *chaises de commodité.* That the chaises were in place by 1681 is important because it establishes their presence in Dauphiné well before the end of the century.[16] We cannot know from the inventory whether local artisans made this type of chair or whether the chair was purchased in Paris or Lyons or elsewhere. But we do know by his notation and description that the notary was familiar with this type of chair and its nomenclature, again suggesting its early availability in the region and its early appearance there.

As noted earlier, the townhouse of Jean de Vincent was fashionably decorated in shades of red and green and his château in a less studied manner; the inventory of this rural residence suggests no overall color scheme at all. The contents of the château were in general less fine than those listed for the townhouse. As previously disclosed, Vincent's collection of silver was located in the townhouse.[17] The preference given the high-profile urban residence over the rural was common among office-holding families in Dauphiné. But found in the rural residence and not in the townhouse were a large *chaise de commodité* (with a down cushion) and a daybed. That these two pieces were located in the château and not the townhouse betokened a different use of the two spaces. In town the family and its residence were on view; in the country residence family members found a more private space, perhaps a bit ramshackle and less decorated, but one that included the most comfortable and innovative furnishings.

The Franquières' townhouse offers another perspective on urban/rural dichotomy. The Franquières' château in the countryside and their townhouse in Grenoble were similarly decorated, but it was in the townhouse that the family chose to showcase its most valuable and fashionable goods. All but six items of Franquières' massive silver collection were located in Grenoble, where they accumulated a large set of silver flatware (marked with various family arms) and the remainder of their extensive silver possessions. The family owned two clocks by Parisian clockmakers and housed both of them in its Grenoble residence.[18] By locating their most costly goods in town the Franquières positioned them for their greatest impact. In this spirit they chose to locate their two sofas in town. There were daybeds in both residences, but only in the inventory of the Grenoble residence does one find reference to sofas. Daybeds had been around much longer; sofas appeared only at the end of the century. No doubt their novelty added to their cachet.[19]

A *cabinet* in the home of Jean Miard, *conseiller du roy* in the chancellery of Dauphiné, served as the location for his *chaise de commodité*. His home was furnished with a predictable array of goods that included as well two daybeds, each located in smaller more interior spaces.[20] And in the apartment of Claude Garcin, attorney for Parlement, the notary listed a *fauteuil de commodité* situated, along with two wingback chairs, in an interior *cabinet*.[21]

By the early eighteenth century the *chaise de commodité* figured in more modest dwellings such as that of Jean-Baptiste Garcin–La Mercière, an attorney to the *bailliage*. His home in Grenoble was outfitted with basic furniture that would not be considered lavish. It did include a *chaise de commodité*, which the notary described as a wing chair made of walnut. It was not heavily padded, and one can assume it was an early version of the chair, possibly with movable parts.[22] This inventory was conducted in 1714; the year before a similar itemization was taken of the contents of the townhouse of Benoît Chalvet, an attorney for the Parlement. Its furnishings were very much the same, including ownership of one *chaise de commodité*, located in a bedroom.[23]

From one notary to the next, the terminology for seating is remarkably the same. Chairs are simply *chaises,* or *chaises à bras,* or occasionally *fauteuils; chaises de commodité* appears to have been used very specifically to refer to easy chairs or reclining chairs. They are sometimes described with wings and sometimes with particularly heavy upholstery and feather cushions, but they are always clearly referenced by the notary as something unique and different from other types of chairs. Daybeds are always referred to as *lits de repos* and sofas unambiguously as simply sofas. The fact of standardization of vocabulary suggests the growing popularity of these items, and certainly the notaries' familiarity with them, a knowledge that clearly extended to other parts of provincial France. Nobles in the Bordeaux region also furnished their homes with *chaises de commodité, lits de repos,* and *canapés* or sofas.[24] Ultimately, elites in Guyenne and Dauphiné acquired more comfortable furnishings because of their fashionable nature.[25]

The period also saw elite homes become more conveniently appointed by the inclusion of more modern means of interior lighting. To date, early modern Europeans had not placed a premium on lighting their dwellings, and, according to Crowley, this had less to do with inventiveness and more to do with cultural values that disdained the need for artificial light as a response to neglected diurnal responsibilities. Even in the homes of wealthy families lighting was extremely limited before the late seventeenth century. The example of Versailles inspired the addition of more candles and lamps to the homes of those with the means to mimic the French court. A stylized use of lighting became a hallmark of design at Versailles. Lighting after sundown made possible a wider range of activities in the evenings, including lit nocturnal socializing and entertaining. From the mid-seventeenth century on, the advantages of extended hours of light became apparent to elite society, and the types of lighting furniture and candleholders in their homes increased steadily. Candlesticks and candelabra increased in number and were used now in pairs; chandeliers, though not commonplace, became popular among elites; and sconces that held multiple candles were used to illuminate and decorate walls.[26] At the same time, consumers also relied on the less attractive alternative to the candle, the oil-burning lamp.

Closely associated with this proliferation of fixtures for lighting was the popularity of the gueridon, or candle stand, which was a small pedestal table that was designed solely for the purpose of holding a candle. Gueridons probably appeared in France around 1650, and their limited size meant easy movement, even in a crowded interior, to the exact point at which lighting was required. Gaming tables, desks, and chairs for reading, for example, were commonly illuminated by an adjacent candle stand. Of basic and simple design, candle stands could have quite elaborate decorative features. Some pedestals were carved in human form to resemble figures from mythology; others portrayed Moors holding trays above their heads; some were designed simply as columns. Often they were decorated with marquetry and sometimes more elaborately with gold gilt. It was not uncommon to find them in sets or designed en suite to accompany a specific table.[27] Whether the gueridon was elaborately carved, adorned or not, its cardinal feature was its capacity to support an illumination source wherever it was needed.

The mirror, as it became more commonplace during the late seventeenth and eighteenth centuries, was closely related to these changes in lighting. Apart from its obvious utilitarian and vanity purposes, the mirror reflected light in ways that enhanced illumination and, perhaps more important, created a rather dramatic effect. "By setting up a play of lights that seemed to expand space, these mirrors embellished interiors, that were often badly lit and excessively cramped, with a touch of wonder and enchantment."[28] Versailles, of course, inspired the coordinated use of candle fixtures and mirrors. For a long time the Venetian glassmakers monopolized the mirror market, but after 1660 both the English and French governments promoted production in these countries, and access increased dramatically. By the eighteenth century, mirrors were no longer a traditional luxury. Many homes included toiletry mirrors, but the mirrors that were essential to the décor were framed and hung on a wall or were pier glasses, that is, fixed between two piers in the wall (fig. 4.2).[29]

All the fixtures and conveniences associated with improved lighting were in evidence in the noble homes of Dauphiné. Notaries routinely listed candlesticks, flambeaux, candelabra, oil lamps, gueridons, and mirrors. Sconces, on the other hand, appeared to have been significantly less common, even rare. The Franquières' château reflects these shining improvements in lighting. In a room that served as a study (it included part of the family's library, a desk, a backgammon game, a clock, among other things), the inventory lists twelve large silver candlesticks and two smaller ones. In the kitchen were a pair of brass candelabra. An adjacent salon/dining room displayed a pair of candlesticks in silver plate. The household was also outfitted with a modest number of mirrors and candle stands. The array of similar objects was, expectedly, much more impressive in the family's home in Grenoble. Consistently this family outfitted its urban dwelling in a more elaborate and au courant manner. Listed among its silver possessions were, for example, fourteen candlesticks, each adorned with the family's coat of arms. The family also owned a pair of silver sconces, six gueridons (some designed to accompany a table), and an impressive array of mirrors. Several of the mirrors had gilded frames, and a couple had pediments marked with the family insignia.[30]

In the Vincent townhouse the list of light fixtures and candle stands was similiar. Despite the fact that Vincent died nearly three decades earlier, in 1691, his household possessions were much the same as those of the Franquières. In the kitchen there were a candelabrum and an oil lamp, each in brass. Another room was outfitted with a desk and a matching pair of gueridons as well as two additional pairs of gueridons, and an oil lamp. His collection of silver included six candlesticks or flambeaux. At the family's château light was provided by two brass lamps, three iron lamps, four brass candelabra, and four wooden candelabra. To accommodate the need for lighting, the family also owned seven gueridons. What is not recorded in this earlier inventory is any kind of wall mirror.[31] Here again, we find Vincent placing his most expensive and impressive items in the urban residence.

Slightly earlier, in 1679, an inventory for the home of Pierre Gleynat, a simple attorney for Parlement, reflected the same kind of urban/rural

FIGURE 4.2. LOUIS XIV–STYLE PEDIMENT MIRROR

dichotomy. His homes included fewer overall light fixtures, candle stands, and mirrors, and those that are listed were found mainly in his Grenoble residence.[32] Over the period 1680–1720 the numbers of lighting objects increased steadily, though they never reached the proportions discussed by Pardailhé-Galabrun in her study of eighteenth-century Paris. Of course, not all artificial light required a silver candlestick, and it is presumable in this period that people used candles without any kind of apparatus (something impossible to determine because there are no listings of candles in the inventories). Still, we can safely assume that there was some amount of lag time between Paris and the provinces and that the process of illuminating a domicile occurred more slowly on the frontier. Beyond question, families enhanced first the lighting of their urban townhouse, where, no doubt, they entertained more often and now in the evening. For *parlementaires* and government officials the demands of socializing and hospitality were greater in town than in the country, and here these conveniences provided provincial consumers illumination past sunset and beyond.

If the mainsprings of fashion were novelty and innovation, consumers took pleasure in the acquisition of goods that were new, and, in the words of Maxine Berg, the "novelty represented by fashion in the seventeenth and eighteenth century was a challenge to the status quo and an unchanging social order. It was a choice of an individualist over a hierarchical lifestyle: changes and trends would allow private individuals at least a minimal margin of freedom, choice, and autonomy in matters of taste."[33] Among the goods that sustained the consumer revolution were items of a novel nature that did not conform to traditional ideas of luxury, items whose practicality and convenience seemed to place them ambiguously between luxury and necessity. *Chaises de commodité,* daybeds, and sofas were all the products of design innovation and gratified the demand for furnishings that promoted bodily comfort and accommodated the desire for greater privacy. They were not used in private spaces exclusively. In some households they were objects on display; in others they were part of the allure of interior spaces. Their novelty promoted their appeal with provincial consumers.

Early modern ideas about political economy contrasted luxury with its polar opposite, necessity. In the eighteenth century, however, comfort was "increasingly applied to a middle ground between necessity and luxury."[34]

Moreover, the political economy of the period "made it possible for both luxury and necessity to become morally neutral terms."[35] Thus, the luxury debate of the eighteenth century assumed a different tone, less concerned with moral corruption and focused more on incentives to consume. Convenience played a significant role in shifting the debate.[36] Dena Goodman maintains, "As the number of objects in circulation increased along with their diffusion through society, the words 'luxury' and 'necessity' lost both meaning and power."[37] The European consumer revolution pertained not only to traditional luxury goods; it included in England a range of goods with "values of usefulness, civility, and ingenuity."[38] I argue, based on the inventories presented herein, that the same was true of France, where remote parts of the realm included, there was a growing awareness of the body and its relationship to the physical environment on the part of craftsmen and consumers.

Writing about the Dutch in the Golden Age, Jan de Vries categorizes these changing ideas as the Old Luxury, an effort to produce or reproduce grandeur and refinement, and the New Luxury, the purpose of which was comfort and enjoyment and which was directed toward the home and specifically its interior.[39] The New Luxury was not about ostentation and opulence; it was about access to objects that had been designed to advance comfort and whose positioning within the household often obscured them from public view.

Many of the changes associated with the New Luxury and the rise of privacy have been more closely identified with England rather than France. England has long been connected with ideas of comfort and a specific cult of domesticity. In his magisterial study of Englishness, Paul Langford writes of the ways in which the English came to value comfort, hearth, and home. It was widely believed in the eighteenth century that English men and women were significantly more privileged in a material sense than their continental counterparts. Foreigners noted the ample way in which the English furnished their homes. In fact, the "sanctity of the comfortable home was often used to explain the stultifying nature of English sociability." The French were known, in contrast, for their gregarious nature and their talents in hosting various gatherings, most notably the salons, in their homes. In the eighteenth century, values of privacy were contrasted with sociability, and thus the English and the French were compared by contemporaries who commented on manners, ways of living, and national character.[40]

In many quarters these cultural stereotypes remained intact through the eighteenth century (and longer). In 1785 John Andrews published a treatise in which he compared the French and English. He drew a stark contrast between the two nations based on different ideas of convenience, comfort, and neatness and argued that the French "conveniences of dwelling, or travelling particularly, are not comparable to those in England." Pointedly, he wrote that French furniture was "mean and penurious, and generally displays an affectation of ornament and finery that ill atones for the wretchedness of the materials they are made of, and ill supplies the want of neatness." Though he was quick to make an exception for the furnishings of the "gentler classes," the general tone of his remarks was one of contempt, and he criticized the French preference for style over substance and practicality. Further, he wrote, "It is with difficulty our English travellers are able to put up with the slovenliness prevailing throughout most parts of France." Here we have in the late eighteenth century an Englishman confirming Anglo cultural stereotypes about the French: a dirty nation that opted for style over substance.[41]

What emerged from this discussion of national character and manners was a dichotomy that typed the English as clean, practical individuals who valued privacy and comfort and presented the French as sociable, though slovenly, people who were slaves to fashion, who opted always for style and form over comfort, and who lived their lives in very public ways. The discourse of nationalism created these polarities in the context of war and economic competition, and such attitudes toward the French were belied by the fact that by the eighteenth century much of Europe eagerly turned to the French court and French elites for design inspiration. Thornton writes that "by 1670 it was widely recognized that the French had a special talent for contriving elegance and comfortable settings for a civilized existence, and by the end of the century French supremacy in this field was even more evident."[42] Andrews's exception for the "gentler classes" of France acknowledged, albeit reluctantly, this supremacy. French nobles, in Paris and elsewhere, formed the gentler classes of consumers whose acquisitions and preferences revealed that marked talent for combining style and comfort with a desire for a measure of privacy. For art historian Mimi Hellman, "a central mythology of eighteenth-century French culture was based on the claim that domestic environments had never before been so commodiously planned and artfully appointed, and that this superior architectural and decorative sensibility was uniquely and essentially French."[43] Certainly, the French argued their singularity on this basis. In 1764, Charles Jombert published an edition of Etienne Briseux's *Architecture moderne, ou l'art de bien bâtir* in which he argued that the French were distinguished by their buildings and their interiors decorated with "elegance, richness, and *commodité.*"[44] For contemporaries and later historians of the decorative arts, the genius of the French was their ability to create comfortable and yet beautiful interiors, a combination of attributes first evinced in *cabinets* or private spaces and later extended to more public ones.[45]

What drove this need for privacy and comfort when for centuries these notions played little role in the aristocratic household? What led French elites to seek comfortable furnishings and private quarters? Perhaps the answer can be found in the very nature of aristocratic culture. Ambition, according to Dewald, was a concept that had become paramount in the cultural milieu of French nobles, and he writes that in the seventeenth century concepts of lineage "performed comforting ideological functions." But another collection of ideas, a contradictory set, was ultimately more important in "defining the French nobility's sense of itself. In describing their lives, nobles spoke less of lineage and ancestry than of personal ambition. They presented themselves as individuals creating their own social positions, rather than as family members growing into positions."[46] In France lives of ambition and public success contrasted with lives of political inefficacy and decay, and residence in the private country home was clearly identified as the result of failure. The French nobility did not produce the country ideology that emerged among English aristocrats, one that envisioned the country house as the site of virtue and a physical manifestation of the continuity between public and private. In France, "nobles had to make their way within the public sphere."[47]

So it is in this context that the idea of privacy and comfort became by the end of the seventeenth century more important and a valued alternative to the public life for the French noble. In a culture of ambition and competition, of hierarchy, clientage, and patronage, and in the world of French polity under Louis XIV, the house became a refuge, and its furnishings, increasingly designed for comfort as well as style, constituted luxuries in a relatively relaxed and secluded environment. By their fashion choices and their appreciation of design innovation, nobles in Dauphiné experienced a kind of freedom and release from the strictures of early modern society. This was the new meaning of luxury at the turn of the century—galvanized by a new desire for privacy, a desire to retreat, albeit briefly and momentarily, from the noble's world of display, ambition and competition.

It would, however, be a gross oversimplification to relegate these new conveniences and furnishings to strictly private space. This is made manifest by their positioning within the Dauphinois households—sometimes in interior spaces but ofttimes in more public spaces. Moreover, the fact that families tended to place these innovative furnishings in the urban homes first also points out that these designs occupied a central place in the décor of sociability and display. The fact that the English commented so critically and contemptuously about the awkwardness of French furnishings, an English mythology about the French, leads us paradoxically to conclude that French ideas of comfort and convenience were to a large extent on display and grossly misunderstood, on display to an audience, foreign and domestic, that did not universally appreciate or understand the French idea of convenience.

Hellman writes about the relationship between furniture design, the body, manners, and sociability in eighteenth-century France. She has argued that furniture of comfort and convenience was itself an actor in social settings, that negotiating these backdrops and knowing how to use innovative furnishings to one's best advantage provided evidence (or lack thereof) of one's refinement and manners. As the relationship between furniture and the body evolved into more accommodating and yet complex arrangements, it became important to occupy and use furniture in a manner both effortless and knowledgeable. For nobles to appear fumbling, uninformed, or clumsy as they conducted themselves in a richly decorated and conveniently appointed room detracted from their personae because in the eighteenth century sympathies within the noble household were based on performance and display. Hellman observes "that the proliferation of complex furniture—and therefore complex sociability—during the eighteenth century was linked to a growing impulse among elites to complicate and privatize the art of conduct, bring it beyond the level of the textually transmittable at a time when conduct guides were widely available to an expanding range of middle class consumers."[48]

Those celebrated private moments, accommodated by more intimate spaces and innovative furnishings, were not wholly about privacy and intimacy. Even then, nobles were often on view in smaller settings and to more limited groups. The difference between exhibition in the sixteenth century and display in the eighteenth century was one of scale, venue, and audience. The focus of sociability and display shifted to the townhouse from the château; the scale tended to smaller groups; and the onlookers were a largely homogeneous gathering of elites. It was this life in the *hôtel* or urban townhouse that seemed so awkward, so inconvenient, so superficial to Englishmen, whose paragons of domesticity were at odds with what appeared to be a still very public way of living. As one Englishman wrote, 'The first thing that strikes a stranger is, that a Frenchman has *no home:* He lives in the middle of the public."[49] By living in "the middle of the public," this critic denotes the paradoxical nature of the noble home in late seventeenth- and early eighteenth-century France. While scaling down the social setting and situating it in smaller spaces, French nobles did not abandon competition and display, and, to the English, such backgrounds were far from cozy.

For the French, no longer was social performance focused on the village, the community, the town; now the audience was limited more to small groups of similarly situated individuals, assembled in smaller settings where one-upmanship had reached a heightened, new level of intensity and in which was required an easy familiarity and facility with the furnishings. For the Englishman, the comfórtable features of French furnishings were not readily apparent; their use demanded a requisite savoir faire to inhabit them in a pleasing and flattering manner. Nor was the French townhouse truly private, except for brief respites, because it too was a setting for performance before a more select group of people. As revealed in the following chapter, the material culture of these homes displayed the fundamental difference between traditional forms of hospitality and the newer sociability that emerged during the reign of Louis XIV and flourished in eighteenth-century elite homes.

À TABLE

DINING AND SOCIABILITY

Nothing is more closely associated with the rise of *la grande nation* than its cuisine. France acquired its reputation as a nation of gastronomes and gourmands during the reigns of Louis XIV and Louis XV, when several legendary French authors published recipes that altered the way in which food was prepared and presented, first among French elites and, later, internationally. Early modern cookbooks played a pivotal role in changing food preparation from the medieval style to that of classic French cuisine, a transformation that earned France its historical reputation as a nation of culinary authority. Inventing a cuisine that was more expensive, more subtle, more labor-intensive, and more systematic, La Varenne and others laid the foundation for the grand culinary tradition of France.

Food distinguished provincial hosts and hostesses by establishing them as the arbiters of good taste, and their appetite for dishes produced by new recipes and techniques was another way in which they were influenced by and drawn into the culture of the court and the Parisian aristocracy. The noble homes of Dauphinois are evidence that this new style initiated by La Varenne and developed by others caught on quickly. By serving the new style of cuisine provincial nobles conveyed their appreciation of this food and exhibited an all-important capacity for good taste. As approaches to cooking changed, so did the role of host and hostess, this as a result of the decline of medieval forms of hospitality and the rise of more modern forms of sociability. These changes complemented and promoted the culinary revolution.

The medieval cooking paradigm was based on ancient theories of health and the body. Cooks tried to promote a healthy balance of the essential humors by the preparation of crucial foods consumed for the benefits of their supposed therapeutic qualities. Color and appearance were particularly important. Color more than taste distinguished dishes for the medieval cook and diner. Fewer dishes were served, and many recipes involved a predictable array of heavy spices, so their appearance was paramount. Spinach juice or parsley produced a bright green; egg yolk and saffron transformed dishes into shades of yellow; red was harder to effect but generally came from sunflowers; and gold and silver leaf conspicuously garnished dishes at banquets. To accentuate form, cooks created elaborate shapes in pastry. Or by sewing a cooked bird back into its feathered skin, the cook made it resemble its living self.[1]

As a rule, the medieval banquet table was laden with meats and low on vegetables. Meats were simply prepared by boiling or roasting them (roasting whole pieces of meat was generally limited to the privileged segments of society). The medieval paradigm did not distinguish between sugar and salt. Meats and fishes could be salted or prepared with fruits or sugar, which were believed to stimulate the appetite. Sour and bitter flavors were also standard. Vinegar was used in the cooking of meats, as was verjuice, an acid-flavored liquid derived from the juices of unripened grapes or crab apples. Sauces were strongly flavored and often bitter to conceal blandness or noisesomeness. This method of preparation was, of course, the reason for and source of the famous spice trade with Asia: to procure the cinnamon, cloves, nutmeg, mace, cumin, cardamom, and coriander necessary to flavor the meats and stews concocted in the medieval period.[2]

The sixteenth century saw previous ideas about food preparation and consumption change in ways that laid the foundation for La Varenne. Broadly speaking, these changes can be attributed to printing, to the growing interest in diet among educated individuals, and to the importance of dining at court. Although a couple of important cookbooks were written in the medieval period, it was the onset of printing that ensured the rise of the modern cookbook and the audience that was crucial to the cultivation of classic French cooking. Printing also promoted greater awareness of food and diet among educated segments of society. The publication of classical works that frequently made mention of a relationship between diet and health heightened awareness and surely elevated the importance of food as a topic for discussion in educated circles.[3]

At the same time, French contact with Italians and Italian court culture grew and shaped the ways in which courtiers and monarchs dined. The appearance in Italy in 1475 of Platina's *De Honesta Voluptate,* which included a collection of recipes, was important for a number of reasons. Important among them was the fact that it legitimated food and diet as a topic for polite and educated society through its ideas and by its humanistic reliance on classical authors. Italian court cooks anticipated the rise of French classical cooking by placing less emphasis on meat and more on vegetables, fruit, pastries, soups, and charcuterie. But their direct impact on French cooking has been questioned.[4] For Barbara Ketcham Wheaton, too much significance has been attached to the arrival of Catherine de Medici at court. She argues that the Italian influence predates this event, sustained by a variety of different contacts, with Catherine's impact not so much on cookery but on the production of festivals and the etiquette of dining.[5] Susan Pinkard agrees that attributing the changes in cuisine to the arrival of Catherine de Medici is one of "the evergreen myths of culinary history," and she further argues that food at court during this period remained essentially medieval in its style of preparation.[6]

In France it was the publication of La Varenne's *Le cuisinier françois* in 1651 that marked the true departure from medieval cooking. What is it that defined his style as distinct from medieval cookery and established the prototype of French classical cuisine? Food historians comment on the fact that in *Le cuisinier françois* cooking became significantly more systematic, depending on a few fundamental components upon which many recipes were based. These included bouillon or stock, liaisons, farces, bouquet garni, and the roux. *Le cuisinier françois* retained many medieval recipes and introduced new ones defined by a different cooking method with resulting differences in texture and flavor. The new dishes generally were not seasoned with the heavy spices that made medieval dishes taste so substantially like one another. La Varenne relied instead on the bouquet garni of herbs so closely associated with classic French cooking. There was now less meat and more vegetables, including many recipes incorporating asparagus, cauliflower, and artichokes, and meat recipes tended to be less exotic. La Varenne produced a sauce anticipating the modern hollandaise and is credited with the invention of the recipe for duxelle (the mushroom, shallot, and butter combination), though the latter is not actually found in his book.[7]

Le cuisinier françois represented a major break with the past and marked the beginning of a culinary revolution carried on by succeeding cookbook authors and chefs. Pierre de Lune published *Le cuisinier* in 1656; L.S.R. (known by his or her initials) published *L'Art de bien traiter* in 1674; and Massialot published *Le cuisinier roial et bourgeois* in 1691. These crucial works, together with La Varenne, inspired many emblematic developments in French haute cuisine: the butter-based sauce that replaced verjuice and the acidic sauces of the Middle Ages; the use of herbs, especially parsley and thyme, in place of the medieval spices; and a general simplicity and delicacy in the recipes that came to define haute cuisine.[8] The new style also involved the salient separation of salt and sugar, saving the latter for dishes served at the end of the meal. Here the French may have been inspired by the Italians and some ancients, who had argued that sweetness suppressed or dulled the appetite. Salt was elevated to a new position of prominence in cooking, and pepper also came to occupy a central place in French cuisine. Over time, they were used more and more in tandem.[9]

Among La Varenne's successors, Pinkard argues for one author's special importance in defining the new cuisine. In the 1650s Nicolas de Bonnefons published *Les Délices de la campagne* and *Le Jardinier françois*. Together these books made the goal of the cook *le gout naturel*—to enhance the simple flavor of the principal ingredient—rather than layering on complex spice mixtures that profoundly changed its taste. The new goal was to highlight the flavor of that ingredient rather than change or mask it.[10] This resulted in a relatively simple cuisine that involved the best seasonal products and ushered in a new form of conspicuous consumption. The best seasonal products that the farm and countryside could produce became a new luxury.[11]

The cooking fashion required intimate familiarity with the recipes that were its basic building blocks, and it required a kitchen outfitted with the standard, appropriate hardware and utensils. It is clear that the well-equipped kitchen included an essential *batterie de cuisine.* Many of these items derived from the Middle Ages, but the list of requisite utensils increased significantly in the later seventeenth century. Medieval cooking had taken place over a fireplace, where meats were boiled or roasted, and an important piece of equipment was the *cremaillière,* or pot hook, from which was suspended a large iron caldron. This utensil continued to play a central role through the eighteenth century, in part because cooks still performed their craft using a fireplace. Wrought-iron grills had also been important to the medieval cook, as was the *lechefrite,* or dripping pan.[12]

The early modern kitchen was more elaborately outfitted and included a much wider array of pots, pans, and skillets in copper, brass, or iron. Sean Takats points out that by the eighteenth century the *batterie de cuisine* had become an index of the owner's wealth.[13] State-of-the-art cooks preferred tinned copper cookware. In *L'Art de bien traiter,* signed simply with the initials L.S.R. and published in 1674, the author lays out for the reader exactly what equipment is needed to produce the tastes and dishes described therein.[14] The author's list included:

—stockpots of several sizes in cast iron and tinned copper, with the largest one being used for bouillon
—ceramic pots in various sizes
—terrines and *huguenots*
—tinned copper pans and lids, both oval and round
—large and small caldrons in brass
—pewter bowls
—*poissonières,* long, round and oval
—pie or tart dishes/pans with covers
—tin molds, oval and round, for small pâtés
—molds for biscuits and pastry
—pans for fricassee frying, and for chestnuts
—spatulas
—skimming ladle
—wooden spoons
—colanders

—rolling pins
—spits for the fireplace
—copper cisterns, one for drinking water and one for washing
—a pot hook/trammel
—caster iron and ceramic cloches
—pan for confiture
—chafing dishes or burners

With few exceptions, here are the pots, pans, and utensils referred to earlier by La Varenne throughout the corpus of his work.[15] His *batterie de cuisine* included the standard medieval equipment and also strainers, skimmers, and colanders. These devices permitted him to strain the bouillon from the meats and vegetables whose essence had been distilled into rich stock that was the foundation for sauces associated with French haute cuisine. It is the variety of pots and pans, their appearance in tinned copper, and the emergence of a wide range of skimmers and strainers that technologically defined the new style.[16] Copper cookware was not new, but in the early modern period it replaced iron in many well-equipped kitchens.

In Paris eighteenth-century kitchens were furnished first with a view for cooking over the fireplace, where most cooking still took place. Andirons, trammels or pothooks, grills, trivets, and burners were basic. Spits and machines to turns spits enabled cooks to roast meat evenly by easy turning. Pots and pans were plentiful, and over the century they were relegated to specific tasks; there were pans for sauces, pans for omelets, pans for frying, pans for jam, and pans for pies. The same was true of pots—stock pots, fruit-cooking cloches, braising pots, *poissonières,* and kettles (*coquemars*). Tools included sieves, skimmers, mortars, pestles, cleavers, scales, and a variety of spoons.[17]

Dauphinois homes were outfitted similarly. Inventories of elite homes list the same items in their kitchens; indeed, the list becomes entirely predictable from one home to the next. The Franquières' households each included a *batterie de cuisine* both impressive and indicative of the styles of cooking that had penetrated to the remoter parts of the realm.[18] In their château, the kitchen was outfitted with the following:

—one pair of scales
—one jack for turning the spit

—two *attières*
—a trammel or pot hook
—a large set of andirons
—two large pots of iron
—two copper warming pots
—two fruit cloches
—four large copper kettles or caldrons
—one copper *poissonière*
—two copper saucepans
—two dripping pans
—four tin plate covers
—one brass strainer
—one copper mixing bowl
—one grill
—two small spits
—two skillets
—one iron trivet
—one copper cistern

The Franquières *hôtel* in Grenoble was even more elaborately outfitted:

—two copper bowls
—five copper kettles
—one copper cistern
—three copper pie or tart pans (along with their covers)
—one small copper pie or tart pan
—six copper saucepans
—five copper skillets
—one iron jack for turning the spit
—two dripping pans
—one pan for frying
—five iron pots
—two *attières* of iron
—two trammels
—two iron andirons
—two burners
—three grills
—one copper coffee pot
—one cleaver

—two graters
—one nut press
—one scale
—one iron skimmer
—one rolling pin

This list was standard, and most households inventoried maintained kitchens filled with the same equipment. Clearly there were differences in scale, that is, in numbers, but the basic elements and components of cooking stayed much the same from one place to the next, suggesting that by the 1680s or thereabouts there was a clearly identifiable *batterie de cuisine* in noble homes. The same pots, pans, and accessories equipped the noble households around Bordeaux.[19] Actually, from the point of view of culinary technology there is no evidence of regional distinctiveness. Obviously, a pot or a kettle would be the same from one province or region to another, and the terminology for all this cookware was the same from Bordeaux to Grenoble.

How did such a standard vocabulary describing similar inventories exist from one region to the next? This model seems to run counter to the deeply entrenched regional or provincial cultures and cuisines long recognized in France. What about Charles de Gaulle's famous remark concerning the difficulties in governing a country with 246 different types of cheese? In part, standardization arose from the publication of the great cookbooks. La Varenne's *Le cuisinier françois,* for example, was published first in 1651 and then frequently thereafter for the next century. Widespread access was ensured by the fact that this seminal culinary manual was printed as part of the cheap *bibliothèque bleue* offerings. Later cookbooks would be published in even greater volume. Still, despite the profusion of copies, cookbooks are rarely found in the inventories of libraries or estates, for the simple reason that they were not likely to last very long because of their constant and certain abusive use in the kitchen.[20] Of ten thousand inventories in eighteenth-century Franche-Comté, only twenty-nine record cookbooks.[21] In a rare instance of preservation, the importance attached to these cookbooks is shown by the fact that Pierre de Ponnat kept one copy of *Le cuisinier françois* at his home in Grenoble and a separate volume at his country house.[22]

The library of Jean de Vincent also included duplicate copies of *Le cuisinier françois*. His kitchen was equipped with all the items listed above, leading us to the conclusion that the servants working in his kitchen were encouraged to cook in the modern way.[23] For them to do so, it would have provided great facilitation had the cook been able at least to read, if not write. Of course, we cannot make this assumption based solely on the fact that cookbooks appeared in the library of the head of the household. Still, it is surely conceivable that the cooks at the Vincent and Ponnat residences did read *Le cuisinier françois*. Takats has written persuasively to argue the literacy and numeracy of eighteenth-century cooks in Paris, whose job required them to maintain inventories and account books. "Kitchens were sites of writing and calculation; pen and account book were two of cooks' most important tools."[24]

The popularity of these early cookbooks extended to other countries owing in large part to the fact that haute cuisine, as the term would suggest, was class based. La Varenne's revolutionary volume was translated and published in English as *The French Cook* after only two years in 1653; it appeared in German in 1665; and the Italian translation came out in 1682. What generated this strong international demand for the book and the new style of cooking that it promoted? Although cuisine would ultimately become a topic of nationalistic discourse and pronouncements, in the early modern period it was a topic most closely aligned with class interests. "In the seventeenth and eighteenth centuries, *French*—as in French cuisine—made less of a geographical reference than a social statement."[25]

The recipes in the books of La Varenne and his successors were prescriptive. As Priscilla Parkhurst Ferguson describes their role, "Insofar as cookbooks legislate rather than document, they necessarily construct cuisine *against* practice, which it aims to constrain and contain."[26] Thus constructed as instructed, haute cuisine was intended for courtly and aristocratic society, and there it flourished, extending to the courts and manor houses of different parts of Europe.

The courtly origins of the revolution in cuisine is a matter of debate. Pinkard finds that the menus at Louis XIV's Versailles were actually conservative and reflected his preference for heavily spiced recipes that were essentially throwbacks.[27] It was Paris that provided an audience for the new cookbooks. Here elite society, whose self-image rested on the idea of connoisseurship, embraced the new way of cooking as part of the larger refashioning of the nobility then occurring. For Pinkard the great impetus for this revolution in cuisine came from Parisian high society and not from Versailles.[28]

The international reach of French cookbooks and chefs was soon apparent in Britain, where many households of the aristocracy included a French chef. If lacking a French chef in residence, a family of sufficient means sent the head of its kitchen to France for the proper training.[29] The impact of French cuisine on the British aristocracy was so profound that in 1753 an Englishman lamented its impact on dining among the powerful and argued its sinister effects on British society. "Now you cannot Dine with a great Man, but you will have in every Dish on the Table, some little *French* Kickshaws,[30] where the Flesh is so disguised, that it puzzles an ordinary Capacity to discover what the Ground-work is; whilst the old *English* Sir Loin is banished to the Side-board. We know not but that this great Alteration of our Food and *French* Cooks (with the Assistance of *French* Taylors, *French* Peruque-makers, and *French* Valets) has propagated the *French* Interest as much as any Thing else, except the *French* Gold. For if our Nutriment be according to our Food, we know not but that eating thus always *French* makes us think and act *French*."[31]

Echoing this protestation that French cuisine had become synonymous with eating well among British elites, Joseph Addison reported in *The Tatler* that he had been invited to dine at the home of a friend known to have been a great admirer of French cuisine and as someone who "eats well." Addison found the table to be covered in dishes with which he was completely unfamiliar. He mistakenly took a larded turkey for a porcupine. Addison described his bewilderment *à table:* "I was now in great hunger and confusion when, methought, I smelled the agreeable flavor of a roast-beef, but could not tell from which dish it arose, though I did not question but it lay disguised in one of them. Upon turning my head, I saw a noble sirloin on the side-table smoking in the most delicious manner. I had recourse to it more than once, and could not see, without some indignation, that substantial English dish banished in so ignominious a manner, to make way for French kickshaw."[32] What was an Englishman to do? Here we see the conflict that occurred within educated and elite Britons who struggled to reconcile personal preferences with style, and style with national identity. Even the positioning of dishes made clear that the traditional English roast beef had been relegated to second-rate status. French culinary hegemony was not an easy pill to swallow; nonetheless, appreciation of French cuisine was now embedded as an essential part of an international elite culture defined in part by its palate and taste for this style of cooking.

Comments like these illustrate that the elite origins and international popularity of French cuisine may have played a role in shaping French nationalism and Frenchness. And they show that the style of cooking preferred by elites probably served as a preliminary step on the road to a truly national cuisine. Food historian Ken Albala contends that national cuisines originate on top for political reasons rather than as a "grass-roots accumulation of tradition practices." But this does not preclude indigenous origins and elements in a national style of cooking. It does mean that a style of cooking is national if it has been identified as such both inside the nation and beyond and in turn implies that the "process of codifying a national cuisine always involves excission [*sic*] of everything that refuses to follow the national model, whether the product of native soil or not."[33]

Haute cuisine served nobles, even in the provinces, as a way to distinguish themselves from the bourgeoisie and the upwardly mobile families that aspired to the noble status and lifestyle. It provided another degree, or more, of separation. Jean-Louis Flandrin points out that the cookbooks themselves made this clear by pointedly attacking the old ways of cooking as bourgeois.[34] They rapidly became an international lexicon for good taste, and one that always acknowledged its French origins. If color and appearance had reigned supreme in medieval cooking, taste, or good taste, was the guiding principle for early modern chefs. For a dish to taste good, the diner must have the ability, the good taste, to appreciate it as a good tasting dish.[35] Taste therefore became another mark of nobility, and in the process appreciation of haute cuisine became a mark of Frenchness.

This discerning relationship between elites and food did not begin in France, and, of course, it was never limited to elites in France. Certainly by the late Renaissance in Italy, it is apparent that elites were engaging food in new ways. Gone was the medieval banquet with its large quantities of heavily spiced food devoured by people with great relish and enthusiasm but without exhibition of the behavior associated later with connoisseurship and taste. Savoring the fine points of the meal and a more subtle style of cooking inspired a new food ideology associated with elites. "Appreciating the proper balance of spices, or the perfect degree of cooking by the most complex methods invented, ran in tandem with good taste in paintings and poetry."[36]

Takats sees a fundamental and epistemological difference between cookbooks written in the seventeenth century and those that appeared later in the eighteenth century. Earlier authors like La Varenne attributed their culinary success and innovation to the inspiration provided by the good taste and superior example of their employers. The key was a sort of secret knowledge that came from exposure to elites. "Taste originated with elites, and cooks learned taste either from serving with sophisticated masters or from gaining this knowledge via cookbooks."[37] In contrast, later cookbooks placed more emphasis on the innovative cook as the source of good taste. Novelty and obsolescence became the inspiration for new cookbooks and new recipes.[38] By the eighteenth century much had been written about good taste, and much had been written about good taste as an indication of the inner man.[39]

Medieval concepts viewed sedulous aristocratic hospitality and the tradition of good lordship conclusive evidence of nobility. Hospitality was a form of largesse in which all social groups in the community were invited to dine at the open house of the local lord. The lord's residence was open to the poorest members of the community, even to passersby, and thereby composed an act of Christian virtue. Indeed, hospitality was an important form of charity and was considered the "queen of medieval virtues." According to Felicity Heal, "The idea of an indissoluble link between gentility and household generosity was ... reinforced by the argument that liberality was the particular prerogative of gentlemen and one of the most visible manifestations of true, that is inner, nobility."[40] Aristocratic hospitality as an act of charity was clearly associated with the poor. At the same time, it was an important means by which nobles demonstrated their power to the local community.[41]

Hospitality, sometimes to the point of indebtedness, reinforced the power of the local lord by demonstrating his beneficence to those beneath him.[42] The extent and lavishness of his hospitality, of course, depended on his resources and the reasons for such display, which itself had been the mainspring of aristocratic hospitality from the Middle Ages forward. The intended audience was the most important factor shaping the tradition of hospitality. The medieval audience was inclusive and had contained all social groups in the local community. In later times, the audience changed significantly. Elites no longer hosted the entire spectrum of society, rich to poor, that had formed the guest list in medieval and Renaissance times. Instead, the lists of invited shrank as increasingly they hosted at home only their own social stratum. By the eighteenth century, nobles entertained their peers in smaller, more intimate gatherings that contrasted dramatically with the raucous medieval banquet hall. Quite simply, medieval forms of hospitality gave way to early modern sociability rituals. Sociability involves social equals, and it promotes gentility by means of exclusivity. Elite social rituals evolved into more exclusive and genteel forms as elite society withdrew from popular culture over the course of the early modern period. This process was clearly under way by the reign of Louis XIV. Did changes in cooking drive changes in social rituals and elite society or did changes in elite society drive changes in cooking? If we listen to La Varenne, it was the good taste of patrons that served as inspiration for this major social and cultural shift.

The transition from medieval to early modern rituals included the rise of the salon and its attendant supper. In the seventeenth century the salon, a small gathering for the purpose of discussing literature and philosophy, became an important form of aristocratic sociability. The salon dates from the early seventeenth century, and again the Marquise de Rambouillet played a formative role. As trendsetter, she became the first important *salonnière*. For decades her home, the celebrated *Chambre bleue,* was the scene of intimate gatherings of Parisian aristocrats and intellectuals. These evenings were marked by their free-flowing nature, by the fact that strictures of rank applied at court did not apply in the salon, where the spontaneous expression of ideas trumped stolid hierarchy. Closely related to the salon was the dinner party, a new type of sociability associated with the revolution in cooking that was taking place simultaneously.[43]

In his study of the salons in eighteenth-century Paris, Antoine Lilti finds a central role played by gastronomy and the table.[44] Dining and the "pleasures of the table" were by then closely associated with elite sociability. As Lilti points out, the expression "aller souper" was both au courant and revealing in that it reflected the major role played by the meal in salon society. Not all guests opted to dine, but they all used the expression to indicate their plans to attend the intimate evening experience. The great *salonnières* directed their staffs to prepare service for approximately two dozen guests, though, as a rule, only half of these actually chose to dine. Menus reflected the revolution in cuisine and were distinguished by their simplicity. Certain *salonnières* were known for their signature menus. Madame Geoffrin was closely associated with the spinach omelet that she routinely offered. For Madame de la Vallière it was lentils. In other circles, menus might be more or less elaborate but always reflected the changes in cooking that came to define French cuisine. Madame Vigee-Lebrun favored a menu of chicken, fish, a platter of vegetables, and a salad.[45]

In the transition from the medieval banquet to the eighteenth-century salon, the presentation and service of food were essential. During the reign of Louis XIV hosts in France and elsewhere embraced the systematic table setting known as *service à la française*. The basic principle of this style was service from the table itself with a number of choices within each course served. The number of dishes was based on the dishes-to- diners ratio, and to accommodate more diners the cooks prepared more dishes. Larger numbers also meant more choices for each course rather than simply increased amounts of a more limited number of offerings.[46] Dishes were arranged on the table so that the diners could serve themselves and those seated near them. Servants were not omnipresent in the more intimate settings, and diners served themselves and each other from dishes that were situated within easy reach. Serving soup and fish and carving meat were tasks of distinction and accomplishment reserved for the host and hostess.[47] Ease of access was not the only guiding principle; the actual arrangement of dishes was one of geometric precision in which foods were organized symmetrically and by size. Wheaton offers an example of a small supper served on a square table with a soup tureen at the center: "The corners of the table would be occupied by four medium-sized platters, each with a different delicacy; four small plates would be placed between the large ones. The pattern would be completed with eight small dishes set round the outside of the main body of the course—these are the hors d'oeuvre (in this first phase of development, spatially, not temporally, outside the main body of the meal)."[48] La Chapelle included in his cookbook, *Le cuisinier moderne* (1742), an illustration of such a meal (fig. 5.1).[49]

What menu might be served with this arrangement? François Massialot proposed a number of menus, including this one for twelve people to be served in the month of January:

The First Course

POTAGES AND SIDE-DISHES

Two Potages:
one a bisque of pigeon and the other Capon with root vegetables

Partridge Pie

Chicken with Truffles

THE GREAT DISH IN THE MIDDLE

Two pieces of Roast Beef, garnished with cutlets of fried veal and a good sauce

FOR THE OUT-WORKS

A poupeton of Pigeons

A dish of quails broiled under the coals

A dish of farced chicken, with the strained liquor of mushrooms

The Second Course

THE ROAST MEAT

Turkey garnished with partridges, chickens, wood-cocks and mauviettes

Quarter of Lamb garnished in the same manner

THE INTERMESSES

A cream-tart for the great Dish in the middle, garnished with puffs,
feuillantins, fleurons and milk beignets or fritters

Pain au Jambon garnished with small toasts of bread and lemon

Gammon of Bacon and other salt-meats

THE OUT-WORKS

Blanc-manger

Liver of Capons

Asparagus in a Salad

Truffles in a court-bouillon

The Third Course

FRUITS AND CONFITS[50]

The diner seated before this elaborate arrangement had at his or her place a plate, fork, spoon, and, perhaps, a knife. Individual place settings had replaced the use of communal cutlery, bowls and trenchers, and was a hallmark of the new etiquette that accompanied the neoteric way elites lived and dined. They served as another social marker to separate elites from those beneath them. They also reflected a growing consciousness and concern with cleanliness.[51] It was the Italians who first used individual forks, in the sixteenth century, which encouraged the development of the individual plate to replace eating from the medieval communal bowl. The earliest forks were two tined, and later in the seventeenth century three- and four-tined forks began to appear.[52] Individual knives existed in the period but were not common, prompting Pardailhé-Galabrun to speculate that guests brought with them their own knives, which they ostensibly carried with them at all times.[53] Glasses were not generally part of the table setting until much later. Instead, servants brought glasses and served wine when the diner was ready; otherwise, glasses, bottles, and decanters were not present on the tabletop.[54]

To navigate *à table* there was a prescriptive literature on etiquette and civility that addressed the details of dining, the use of utensils, and other aspects of comportment at meals. One of the most popular etiquette manuals was Antoine de Courtin's *Nouveau traité de la civilité qui se pratique en France, parmi les honnêtes gens* (1671), which was reprinted and translated many times. He clearly specified what the polite man or woman did with utensils and what was no longer permissible. A concern for hygiene and

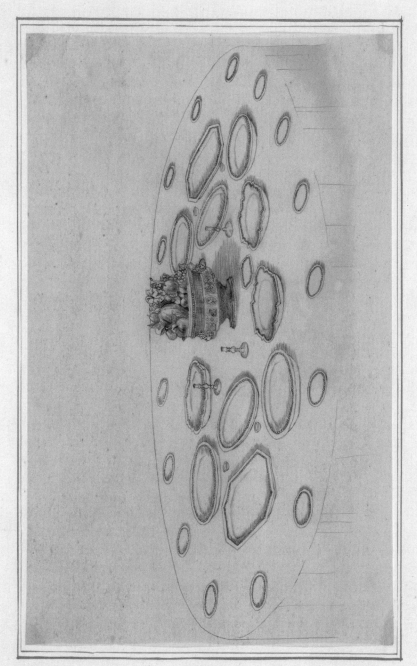

FIGURE 5.1. TABLESCAPE PROPOSED BY LA CHAPELLE

appearance is clear. No food except bread is to be picked up or touched with the hands. A spoon used to taste something must not be then used in the tureen to serve. Courtin was not wholly concerned with cross-contamination of dishes, since he found it curious that some people were so fastidious as not to allow a spoon to serve from two separate dishes: "Tis grown a Mode to have Spoons brought in with every Dish to be used only for Pottage and Sawce." Then there was the Scylla and Charybdis of the napkin. To use or not to use. Courtin cautioned between using the napkin for the appropriate purpose and using it to the extent that it becomes "as nasty as a Dish-Clouth, and . . . nauseates the Company." His advice for the unfortunate and clumsy diner who has dirtied his or her fingers: "If you wipe them not upon your Napkin, you must do it upon your Bread, and if not upon your Bread, you must lick your Finger, which is the worst way, and the most uncomely of the three."[55] Finally, he offered some insight into the delayed appearance of the glass at the individual table setting. He discouraged one from sipping leisurely his or her wine, arguing that "it savours of too much Familiarity to sip your Wine at the Table, and to make three or four Draughts before you come at the bottome: 'Tis better to drink it off at once, not rambling up and down the Room with your Eyes, but keeping them fix'd at the bottom of the Glas; nor tumbling it into your Throat as into a Tun; that would be liker a Drunkard than a Gentleman."[56] It appears that chugging one's wine had not yet become the faux pas that it would be later.

Furnishings for entertaining and for tablescapes proliferated during this period, just as recipes became more numerous and the basic design of menus more elaborate. Beyond the fundamentals of individual place settings (the knife, fork, spoon, and plate), the period saw more ornate and beautiful vessels for serving food and drink. By the designs and positioning of serving pieces, the table itself became a work of art. The backdrop for artful presentation of food was, of course, the tablecloth. Napery included tablecloths, napkins, and hand towels, and damask was especially popular.[57] It was customary to fold napkins in the shapes of animals, and La Varenne provides his readers with instructions on how to transform the napkin into pheasants, capons, cows, fish, turtles, and rabbits, to name a few.[58] Nobles outfitted their homes with extensive collections of table linens and other textiles, a pattern that extended beyond France and Europe in general to the American colonies. In the seventeenth century tablecloths were often layered on top of a family's precious table carpet as protection.[59]

Service à la française required greater numbers of vessels and serving pieces because the number of dishes and choices had burgeoned. This in turn presented aesthetic problems. How best to achieve a pleasing effect on the table? One answer was in the geometry and rhythm of the table's arrangement. Another involved the effort to create artistic unity by matching the vessels themselves. Silver was the preferred material, and families often purchased silver items in sets or pairs to balance the table and create a unified effect. If means allowed, they also furnished their tables with complete silver services. In much the same way that the French decorated in a single color to create *regularité*, so they matched their services. Dinners and banquets at Versailles set the trend, and elites in Paris and the provinces followed suit. And as these trends were interpreted, the focus of dining and tablescapes shifted from the buffet or sideboard to the dining table itself. The table setting became much more elaborate, indeed complicated, but at the same time within a more intimate setting.[60]

Covered dishes, cruets for oil and vinegar, and casters were among the components of the tablescape. These pieces originated in Italy, and their use became common in France during the late seventeenth century. Sauces were served from vessels with two handles and two spouts, the prototype of the sauceboat, which represented a major change from the late sixteenth century, when diners dipped bread into simple shallow dishes. Cruets held oil and vinegar with which to dress salads; castors held pepper, dry mustard, and sugar; and the traditional spice box (and its accompanying nutmeg grater) still made its appearance at the table. By the early eighteenth century these elements were no longer strewn across the table but had been collected and unified both decoratively and logistically with the appearance of the *surtout*, a contraption with a place for everything. Soups were eaten from the *ecuelle*, which could be presented with or without a cover.[61] And, of course, soups were served eventually from that most decorative of vessels, the tureen, though there is some debate about when exactly it made its appearance.

In Dauphiné households were always outfitted with tableware in tin and pewter. For many families these were their "everyday" services, and when hosting grander occasions they styled their table with silver cutlery or, in a few cases, completely outfitted it in silver. Earthenware or faïence almost never occurred in the inventories and, when present, were always fashioned as containers for storage. Glass was completely absent from the table, and cups were significantly less numerous than plates.

The household with the most extensive collection of silver for the table, among other things, was that of Ponnat, whose service in his Grenoble home included individual settings of dinner plates in silver:

—five dozen plates
—four bowls
—twelve serving platters
—five ewers
—two port assiettes
—two *ecuelles*
—two pitchers
—six salt cellars
—two saucers
—one chafing dish
—one large bowl
—one chandelier
—twenty candlesticks
—one sugar caster
—one mustard pot
—two large spoons
—one large fork
—one slotted spoon
—two dozen spoons
—two dozen forks
—twelve knives with silver handles
—one large knife with a silver handle
—two goblets
—one set (probably for a child) with a small spoon, fork, and knife

Nearly as large was the collection of silver in the Franquière urban household. Most of these items were engraved with one or another coat of arms, and listed were the following in silver:

—a service of eighteen spoons, sixteen forks, and eighteen knives

—four large platters

—four small platters

—three dozen plates

—two spice boxes

—a set of six spoons and six knives

—two pitchers

—one pepper caster

—one old cup

—three old *ecuelles*

—one sugar caster

—one cruet for vinegar

—three old salt cellars

—one small old salt cellar

—two ewers

—two pepper shakers

—two sugar casters

—two ladles for serving potage

—two ladles for serving ragout

—four serving bowls

—one odd plate

—one spoon, one fork, and one knife

—one mustard pot

—one chafing dish

—two salt cellars

—one oil cruet

Not all Dauphinois households had silver goods, though a majority did, and some had only services of cutlery. The first thing a family purchased in silver was cutlery. Other silver items recorded in the inventories included *gondolles,* goblets, covers for platters, and sets of small spoons for coffee. Silver dinner plates were rare, and the Franquières were unusual in their ownership of them, but a matched dinner service in silver was the height of fashion for those who could afford it. Families of more limited means were able to adorn in some manner their tables with silver, and usually silver was engraved with the armorial of the family. One of the virtues of silver was the opportunity it afforded a family to advertise its antiquity and pedigree by clearly labeling pieces with coats of arms. The popularity of the silver dinner service waned when, beginning in the 1720s, the Chinese began making porcelain armorial services to order.[62]

Individual place settings of silver forks and spoons came in sets of varying size, the largest among the inventories being a service for twenty-four (Ponnat household), but usually these sets varied in size from six to eighteen place settings. Obviously, a family's means set limits on the numbers of place settings it could own, but smaller numbers also tell us these elite families hosted small gatherings, presumably in more intimate settings. Knives appear in much more limited numbers and clearly were not part of the place setting.

Elites in Grenoble and environs entertained often. The abundance of linens in their households, especially napkins, suggests this. Laundering napkins, tablecloths, and various sorts of hand towels was a laborious process, which meant that it could take a set of napery out of commission for several days. After being washed and hung out to dry, napkins and tablecloths were folded and pressed with sharp folds, accomplished either by an iron or with a napkin press.[63] By owning multiple sets, in most cases dozens and dozens, a family would not be caught short on table linens. Generally napkins were in toile or damask cotton, and, more than any other goods, napery dominated the household inventories by virtue of the quantities in which it was owned. In a single wardrobe in the townhouse belonging to Pierre de Ponnat, the notary found eighteen dozen napkins and twelve tablecloths in Venetian cotton, a dozen napkins and two tablecloths in Venetian linen, and thirteen napkins and two tablecloths in damask. Then, in two chests he came across eight linen table cloths, four cloths, and twenty-seven napkins in Flemish cotton, and a set of three dozen Venetian linen napkins and six dozen Venetian cotton napkins, in addition to a number of other odds and ends textiles![64] These astronomical numbers are not unique to the Ponnat household, and they afford us a sense of both the importance of table linens and the frequency with which these families must have entertained.

How did these goods translate into a social event at a noble home in Grenoble? Imagine a dinner for twelve consisting of three courses and, following Massialot's plan, seventeen separate dishes. The table is set with a cloth and napkins in Venetian cotton. Before each individual is a silver plate and silver fork, silver spoon, and perhaps a silver knife. Displayed on the table are platters in silver, bowls, and salt cellars and a mustard pot, all in silver. Guests are served from ewers and pitchers, also in silver. The room and table are lighted by a number of silver candlesticks and a candelabrum. For decorative purposes as well as illumination, the room might have a mirror or two on the wall.

The room itself might not have been designated a *dining* room because the modern dining room did not begin to emerge until the late seventeenth century. The modern concept refers to a room that was exclusively for the purpose of dining. Not until well into the eighteenth century does one find rooms routinely designated for this purpose. That is not to say that the family did not always use the same room and its furnishings for dining but rather that there were not yet rooms so exclusively identified. Moreover, it was possible for the family to change the dining venue according to its space needs or whim. Dining tables per se were only beginning to come into existence, and usually a family's tables served a variety of purposes. Folding tables and folding chairs were popular because they allowed hosts to move the dinner easily from one space to another, and they appeared frequently in inventories. The fact that they could be easily moved and stored made them indispensable, especially for dining in more intimate settings.[65]

What these stocks of kitchenware, silver, and linens reveal is that elite families participated in an international culture, based in France, of food snobbery and refined table rituals, all of which was served up in an exclusive and intimate setting. These early modern foodies' appreciation of the meal brought more than epicurean pleasures—it placed them at the metaphorical table within the national, and international, community of connoisseurs.

CONCLUSION

This book has examined the inventories of elite households and identified some important aspects of their owners' daily lives and social world, not the least significant of which was a gradual shift in lifestyle. What their consumer purchases verify was a passage from the medieval/Renaissance household, furnished austerely in an unstudied manner, often the scene of raucous banquets for the larger community, to a more modern style of interior and sociability. Modern implied an interior that was decorated; it implied style according to a plan. Late seventeenth-century interior decoration relied on color schemes and sets of objects, accented by the strategic placement of splendid and showy goods. The household was one of comfortable furniture and convenient devices. And, as modern it was equipped to entertain heeding new forms of sociability—small groups assembled around elaborately appointed tables enjoying a cuisine for the informed palate and the occasion for conversation among social equals.

By intent, this book is not a study of material culture that rests on the Veblen thesis and the thought that acquisition is foremost the product of a desire to emulate one's social superiors.[1] I do not deny the verity of emulation, but it does not explain all or even most consumerism. Roche's work shows that fashion developed around the twin concepts of novelty and obsolescence, maturing forces in the increasingly rich consumer culture of the late seventeenth and eighteenth centuries. Although I appreciate the role played by the überpatron, Louis XIV, in defining period styles and aesthetics, I do not see fashion itself as regime-bound.

This is not to negate the role of king and court in defining style but to suggest that fashion could and did assume a life of its own, a force at once inspired by royal patronage and propelled by the market and its consumers.

There were serious limits to royal power even under Louis XIV. For some time, historians of seventeenth-century France have written to recount the apparent limits of so-called absolutism.[2] Their works depict a royal authority that radiated to the periphery in terms that are pragmatic, flexible, accommodating, and compromising rather than centralizing, reformist, and doctrinaire. And though Louis and his public relations/design team used furniture novelty and grandeur for political purposes, meaning to enhance power by depicting king and court as the font of design innovation, the adoption of these styles had more to do with social and economic forces, the desire to be in style, than the power of the king. Given the practical limits to royal power, especially at the periphery, possession of Louis XIV–style furnishings did not necessarily radiate the power of the state.[3] Louis controlled luxury production through control of the guilds, and thus his role was formative, and style was an aspect of the power of the state. Still, nobles bought the latest designs because they were fashionable, and here loomed the power of the marketplace.

What was fashionable and state of the art in Paris captured the hearts and minds, and soon the purses, of provincial nobles, connoting a closer relationship between center and periphery than historians of grain prices and market integration have maintained—this because consumption of decorative items had little to do with traditional market forces of supply and demand. Instead, social imperatives, local politics, and fashion spurred elite families in their acquisitiveness, and the publications of the period showed them exactly how to amass.

Fashion had an integrative effect that brought closer the material lives of center and periphery. As a catalyst for the drawing together of disparate parts of the realm, the marketplace of Paris earned for itself a special place. By the eighteenth century, the city, not the palace, was the acknowledged trendsetter. "Paris and not Versailles would be promoted as the capital of the modern, civilised world, as 'the centre where all talents, all arts, and all taste come to perfect themselves and flower,' as one journalist enthused."[4] Embedded in fashion was the incipient concept of taste; ideas of taste in turn instructed a component of a nationalistic discourse that insisted only in France did one find the most refined taste.[5]

Through patronage of artists, control of guilds, and the determination to associate France with the production of luxury goods, it is clear that the monarchy played a formative role in forging a national identity that esteemed the French as inherently talented designers of architecture and furnishings. And the success of this campaign can be measured by the extent to which foreigners were seduced or repulsed by it. The idea of the French genius arose in the seventeenth century, during the reign of the Sun King, and flourished through the eighteenth century at home *and* abroad.[6] Aggressive though it may have been in promoting an identity of aesthetics, the state in no sense accomplished it alone. In this process the nobility collaborated. The belief that the French were ineffably more capable aesthetically than other nations sprang not merely from state political expedience but also from period notions of taste and their close association with nobility. More specifically, it was not the French in this period who possessed the national genius; it was the French nobility. Through nobles' aesthetic choices and the desire to be fashionable, elite consumers carved an image for France that would persist longer, even to the present, than any other myth about *la grande nation*. In this, noblemen and -women were the accomplices of the crown.

Consuming at the frontier, the Dauphinois nobility unknowingly assisted this cultural and national process. When the Franquières shipped clocks from Paris and decorated in the latest colors or with the most commodious furnishings, it was clear to their provincial community that they had long since entered the market of French style and taste. As the Mérindols accumulated a collection of paintings whose subjects ran to the secular and to still-lifes, they consciously constructed an image of their lives and household that set them apart. The Vincents' choice of the cartouche allowed them to make statements about their family and their aesthetic sensibilities in one bold decorative move. The botanical collection at the château of the Perissol-Alleman family surely impressed house guests, servants, and villagers alike. In the family's heyday, rows of orange trees neatly pruned and displayed in wooden boxes had to evoke a sense of grandeur, of the exotic, of French control of the landscape. These noble households had, as consumers, elected to follow Paris and French fashion, and they did so decades after the great assault on their nobility, when the *procès des tailles* was long since over. Many of these noble families like the Franquières or the Ponnats, *anoblis* both, had been the cause of the earlier and legendary problem. It was their land acquisitions that had imposed such an intolerable burden on the Third Estate, and it was these families whose indifference to the public good was decried by the pamphleteers and attorneys.

So, are we to conclude that, having been villainized by these authors, noble families self-consciously plunged into the marketplace to reconstruct their honorable and esteemed lives? In no way do I advance the idea that, decades later, *anoblis* families, bearing the scars of the *procès* and the crown's decisions, opted for retail therapy. Rather, the tax conflict had produced in Dauphiné horizontal solidarities and a legacy thereof, a crucial context in which money and lifestyle became paramount. By the fashionable display of French goods, these Dauphinois households embraced new markers of nobility.

In time taste, fashion, and Parisian trends coalesced to form a single and particular basis of national identity. Material culture and the economic and cultural forces that molded and distributed it were essential to the identity of any nation, in France as in Britain and the American colonies. Amanda Vickery writes that in eighteenth-century England consumption conveyed character and promoted the construction of identity, thereby making "a positive contribution to the creation of culture and meanings."[7] For T. H. Breen a marketplace of British goods helped to define an identity for the American colonists, and the disruption of that exchange set off a violent response.[8] For these and many other historians of material culture, goods were about more than economics. Their possession helped the owner construct an identity. Depending on their type, their origins, and their inspiration, that identity could situate the owner in a larger or smaller community. Breen maintains that a "shared framework of consumer experience" gives shape an imagined community.[9] I have consistently alluded to the formation of an international identity or community for elites, based on the ownership of specific goods, mostly inspired by French design and food. This is one of the most important cultural results of the consumer trends of the period. Yet I have also emphasized the French core of this identity, which points to its very national, rather than international, origins. Is it possible to be both? Is it possible for a *fauteuil de commodité* or *omelette aux épinards* at once to give rise to feelings of national pride and to establish one's connections as part of an imagined international community of elite consumers? In short, I think the answer is yes.

And so in Dauphiné an elite, embattled in the first half of the century, emerged to reconstruct itself in the second half. To the extent that goods linked these families with elites in Paris, England, and North America, goods assisted in proving their ascendancy. At the same time, a material culture that was Parisian, or at least inspired by Paris, encouraged among provincial elites the formation of national identity. A few of these families shopped in Paris, but most bought from local and regional artisans designs that were Parisian in influence. Like their counterparts in Guyenne and elsewhere, the Dauphinois pursued a new material culture. In this way, fashion and the powerful belief in a uniquely French understanding of style may have begun to transform provincial nobles into Frenchmen.

NOTES

INTRODUCTION

1. Neil McKendrick, John Brewer, and J. H. Plumb, *The Birth of a Consumer Society: The Commercialization of Eighteenth-Century England* (Bloomington, 1982).

2. Colin Jones and Rebecca Spang, "Sans-culottes, Sans Café, Sans Tabac: Shifting Realms of Necessity and Luxury in Eighteenth-Century France," in *Consumers and Luxury: Consumer Culture in Europe, 1650–1850,* ed. Maxine Berg and Helen Clifford (Manchester, 1999), 37–62. Jones and Spang survey and rely on a growing literature that addresses problems with the earlier work of Labrousse and Braudel, specifically in their analyses of institutional factors that supposedly limited French economic development. Here Jones and Spang are influenced by David Weir's article "Les crises économiques et les origines de la Révolution française," *Annales: Economies, Sociétés, Civilisations* 46 (1991). See also François Crouzet, "England and France in the Eighteenth-Century: A Comparative Analysis of Two Economic Growths," in *The Causes of the Industrial Revolution in England,* ed. R. M. Hartwell (London, 1967), and Michael Sonenscher, *Work and Wages: Natural Law, Politics, and the Eighteenth-Century French Trades* (Cambridge, 1989). Jones and Sprang also base their more positive assessment of the French economy in the later eighteenth century on recent studies of rising consumption. In addition, see Colin Jones, *The Great Nation: France from Louis XV to Napoleon* (London, 2003), 349–63; Daniel Roche, *The People of Paris: An Essay in Popular Culture in the Eighteenth Century* (Los Angeles, 1987); Daniel Roche, *The Culture of Clothing: Dress and Fashion in the Ancien Régime* (Cambridge, 1994); Annik Pardailhé-Galabrun, *The Birth of Intimacy: Private and Domestic Life in Early Modern Paris* (London, 1991); and Cissie Fairchilds, "The Production and Marketing of Populuxe Goods in Eighteenth-Century Paris," in *Consumption and the World of Goods,* ed. John Brewer and Roy Porter (London, 1993), 228–48.

3. David Parker, *Class and State in* Ancien Régime *France: The Road to Modernity?* (London, 1996).

4. James B. Collins, *Classes, Estates, and Order in Early Modern Brittany* (Cambridge, 1994).

5. A notable exception to this is the beautifully detailed work by Michel Figeac, *La douceur des Lumières: Noblesse et art de vivre en Guyenne au XVIIIe siècle* (Paris, 2001).

6. Roche, *Culture of Clothing;* Daniel Roche, *A History of Everyday Things: The Birth of Consumption in France, 1600–1800* (Cambridge, 2000); Roche, *People of Paris.*

7. Pardailhé-Galabrun, 3–4, 7.

8. Pardailhé-Galabrun, 5.

9. Pardailhé-Galabrun, 6.

10. For discussions of the advantages of qualitative rather than quantitative analysis of inventories, see John Styles, "Product Innovation in Early Modern London," *Past and Present* 168 (2000): 126, and Margaret Ponsonby, *Stories from Home: English Domestic Interiors, 1750–1850* (Aldershot, 2007), 6–7.

CHAPTER ONE

1. Material in this chapter appears in Donna Bohanan, *Crown and Nobility in Early Modern France* (London, 2001), chap. 4, and Donna Bohanan, "Color Schemes and Decorative Tastes in the Nobles Houses of Old Regime Dauphiné," in *Furnishing the Eighteenth Century: What Furniture Can Tell Us about the European and American Past,* ed. Dena Goodman and Kathryn Norberg (New York, 2007), chap. 7.

2. Some of the material in this chapter appears in Bohanan, *Crown and Nobility,* chap. 1.

3. Ellery Schalk, *From Valor to Pedigree: Ideas of Nobility in France in the Sixteenth and Seventeenth Centuries* (Princeton, 1986), 65–74.

4. Schalk.

5. Arlette Jouanna, *Le devoir de révolte: La noblesse française et ka gestation de l'état moderne (1559–1661)* (Paris, 1989), 192–8, 208–10.

6. Norbert Elias, *The Court Society* (New York, 1983), 95–103; Kristen B. Neuschel, *Word of Honor: Interpreting Noble Culture in Sixteenth-Century France* (Ithaca, 1989), 76–77.

7. Roger Chartier, ed., *A History of Private Life* (Cambridge, MA, 1989), 3:163.

8. Jacques Revel, "The Uses of Civility," in Chartier, 3:192.

9. Maurice Magendie, *La politesse mondaine et les théories de l'honnêteté, en France, au XVIIe siècle, de 1600 à 1660* (Paris, 1925), 1:387.

10. Michael Moriarity, *Taste and Ideology in Seventeenth-Century France* (Cambridge, 1988), 190.

11. Moriarity, 85.

12. Moriarity, chap. 4; Jean-Louis Flandrin, "Distinction through Taste," in Chartier, 3:305.

13. Saint-Evremond, *The works of Monsieur de St. Evremond, made English from the French original: with the Life of the author; by Mr. des Maizeaux, . . . To which are added the memoirs of the Dutchess of Mazarin, &c.,* 2nd ed., corrected and enlarged (London, 1728), 3:357. *English Short Title Catalogue. Eighteenth Century Collections Online,* Gale Group, galenet.galegroup .com/servlet/ECCO.

14. Saint-Evremond, 3:357.

15. Flandrin, "Distinction through Taste," 292–94.

16. Flandrin, "Distinction through Taste, 298–99.

17. Jennifer M. Jones, *Sexing La Mode: Gender, Fashion and Commercial Culture in Old Regime France* (Oxford, 2004), 114–17.

18. Jones, *Sexing* La Mode, 116–17.

19. Joan DeJean, *Ancients against Moderns: Culture Wars and the Making of a Fin de Siècle* (Chicago, 1997), 128–29; John Styles and Amanda Vickery, introduction to *Gender, and Material Culture in Britain and North America, 1700–1830,* ed. John Styles and Amanda Vickery (New Haven, 2007), 3.

20. Joan DeJean, *The Essence of Style: How the French Invented High Fashion, Fine Food, Chic Cafés, Style, Sophistication, and Glamour* (New York, 2005), 3.

21. Leora Auslander, *Taste and Power: Furnishing Modern France* (Berkeley, 1996), 31.

22. Simon Schama, *The Embarassment of Riches: An Interpretation of Dutch Culture in the Golden Age* (New York, 1987), chap. 5. See also Simon Schama, "Perishable Commodities: Dutch Still-Life Painting and the 'Empire of Things,'" in Brewer and Porter, 478–88.

23. Jan de Vries, "Luxury in the Dutch Golden Age in Theory and Practice," in *Luxury in the Eighteenth Century: Debates, Desires and Delectable Goods,* ed. Maxine Berg and Elizabeth Eger (London, 2003), 41.

24. John Shovlin, "The Cultural Politics of Luxury in Eighteenth-Century France," *French Historical Studies* 23 (2000), 580–83.

25. Maxine Berg, "New Commodities, Luxuries, and Their Consumers in Eighteenth-Century England," in Berg and Clifford, 66–69; Colin Campbell, "Understanding Traditional and Modern Patterns of Consumption in Eighteenth-Century England: A Character-Action Approach," in Brewer and Porter, 40–57; Lorna Weatherill, "The Meaning of Consumer Behavior in Late Seventeenth- and Early Eighteenth-Century England," in Brewer and Porter, 206–27; Amanda Vickery, "Women and the World of Goods: A Lancashire Consumer and Her Possessions, 1751–81," in Brewer and Porter, 274–301.

26. Roche, *Culture of Clothing,* 41–22.

27. Roche, *Culture of Clothing,* 6.

28. Jean-Baptiste Morvan de Bellegarde, *The Modes: Or, a Conversation upon the Fashions of all Nations* (London, 1735; English translation), 8–9.

29. Françoise Waquet, "La Mode au XVIIe siècle: De la folie à l'usage," *Cahiers de l'AIEF* (1986): 91. I am quoting Waquet's description of the content of Grenaille's remarks.

30. Waquet, 92.

31. Waquet, 93–96.

32. Jones, *Sexing* La Mode, chap. 1.

33. Jones, *Sexing* La Mode, 17.

34. Jones, *Sexing* La Mode, 37–38.

35. Jones's translation of Donneau de Visé, in Jones, *Sexing* La Mode, 38 (*Mercure,* 1673, t. 3: 315).

36. Jones, *Sexing* La Mode, 38. See also Louise Godard de Donville, *Signification de la mode sous Louis XIII* (Aix-en-Provence, 1976), chap. 1.

37. Natasha Coquery, *L'Hôtel aristocratique: Le marché du luxe à Paris au XVIIIe siècle* (Paris, 1998), 87–88, 119–21.

38. Figeac, 127–28.

39. Katie Scott, *The Rococo Interior: Decoration and Social Spaces in Early Eighteenth-Century Paris* (New Haven, 1995), 86.

40. Thorstein Veblen, *The Theory of the Leisure Class: An Economic Study of Institutions* (Fairfield, NJ, 1991). For a discussion of the Veblen thesis, see Colin Campbell, *The Romantic Ethic and the Spirit of Modern Consumerism* (London, 1987), 49–57.

41. For a wonderfully succinct discussion of the various interpretations offered by sociologists and historians, see Maxine Berg, *Luxury and Pleasure in Eighteenth-Century Britain* (Oxford, 2005), 37–40. In addition, see Maxine Berg and Elizabeth Eger, "The Rise and Fall of the Luxury Debates," in Berg and Eger, *Luxury in the Eighteenth Century*, 7–27. A somewhat longer discussion about theories of elite consumption can be found in Woodruff D. Smith, *Consumption and the Making of Respectability, 1600–1800* (New York, 2002), chap. 2.

42. Auslander.

43. Richard A. Goldthwaite, *Wealth and the Demand for Art in Italy, 1300–1600* (Baltimore, 1993), 243. See also Dena Goodman, "Furnishing Discourses: Readings of a Writing Desk in Eighteenth-Century France," in Berg and Eger, *Luxury in the Eighteenth Century*, 71–88.

44. Peter Thornton, *Seventeenth-Century Interior Decoration in England, France and Holland* (New Haven, 1981), 4.

45. Thornton, *Seventeenth-Century Interior Decoration*, 29.

46. Thornton, *Seventeenth-Century Interior Decoration*, 29.

47. Jones, *Sexing* La Mode, 25–28. See also Reed Benhamou, "Fashion in the *Mercure*: From Human Foible to Female Failing," *Eighteenth-Century Studies* 31 (1997): 27.

48. Jones, *Sexing* La Mode, 25–26.

49. Figeac, 47–55, 70–91.

50. J. Russell Major, *Representative Institutions in Early Modern France* (New Haven, 1980), 76–77.

51. Daniel Hickey, *The Coming of French Absolutism: The Struggle for Tax Reform in the Province of Dauphiné, 1540–1640* (Toronto, 1986), 19–20; Major, 77–78. See also Bohanan, *Crown and Nobility*, chapt. 4.

52. Hickey, 153–57.

53. Hickey, 88–92.

54. Hickey, 94–98.

55. The 1602 decision recognized the nobility's immunity from taxation, but it brought significant changes that reduced access to future ennoblement. Future *avocats consistoriaux* would be ennobled only by the king, meaning that their ennoblement would no longer be pro forma. Moreover, families ennobled in the previous forty years had now to provide the Parlement with proof of their nobility. See Hickey, 122, and Bohanan, *Crown and Nobility*, 116.

56. Hickey, 157–58.

57. Alain Belmont, "L'Intégration au royaume par les armes: Le Dauphiné et les guerres en Italie, " in *Dauphiné, France: De la principauté indépendante à la province (XIIe–XVIIIe siècles)*, ed. Vital Chomel (Grenoble, 1999), 109–12.

58. Hickey, 158.

59. Jonathan Dewald, *Aristocratic Experience and the Origins of Modern Culture: France, 1570–1715* (Berkeley, 1993), chap. 1.

60. Hickey, 113–17.

61. Jean Vincent, *Discours en forme de plaidoyé pour le tiers estat de Dauphiné* (Paris, 1598), 41.

62. I have taken definitions of *la patrie* from Sarah Maza, "Luxury, Morality, and Social Change: Why There Was No Middle-Class Consciousness in Prerevolutionary France," *Journal of Modern History* 69 (1997): 222–23.

63. Bohanan, *Crown and Nobility*, 111.

64. Antoine Rambaud, *Plaidoyé pour le tiers estat de Dauphiné* (Lyon, 1598), 68–73.

65. Rambaud, *Plaidoyé*, 68–69, 72–73, 90–91.

66. Maurice Virieux, "Le Parlement de Grenoble au XVIIe siècle: Étude sociale" (thèse de doctorat d'état, Paris, 1986), 53. See also Bohanan, *Crown and Nobility*, 120–21.

67. Virieux. The figure of 10 percent is my calculation based on the family biographies contained in Virieux's work.

68. Bohanan, *Crown and Nobility*, 121.

69. Hickey, 106–7.

70. Hickey, 189.

71. Hickey, 190.

72. Kathryn Norberg, *Rich and Poor in Grenoble, 1600–1814* (Berkeley, 1985), 14–15.

73. Lesley Ellis Miller, "Paris–Lyon–Paris: Dialogue in the Design and Distribution of Patterned Silks in the 18th Century," in *Luxury Trades and Consumerism in Ancien Régime Paris,* ed. Robert Fox and Anthony Turner (Aldershot, 1998). See also Carolyn Sargentson, *Merchants and Luxury Markets: The Marchands Merciers of Eighteenth-Century Paris* (London, 1996), chap. 5; William H. Sewell Jr., "The Empire of Fashion and the Rise of Capitalism in Eighteenth-Century France," *Past and Present* 206 (2010): 91–105.

74. T. H. Breen, "'The Baubles of Britain': The American and Consumer Revolutions of the Eighteenth Century," *Past and Present* 119 (1988): 76, 81.

75. Mary Douglas and Baron Isherwood, *The World of Goods: Towards an Anthropology of Consumption* (New York, 1979), 59–60.

76. Pierre Bourdieu, *Distinction: A Social Critique of the Judgement of Taste* (Cambridge, MA, 1984), 2.

CHAPTER TWO

1. Peter Burke, "Conspicuous Consumption in Seventeenth-Century Italy" in *The Historical Anthropology of Early Modern Italy,* ed. Peter Burke (Cambridge, 1987), 136–38. See also Goldthwaite.

2. Goldthwaite, 208.

3. Goldthwaite, 249.

4. Goldthwaite, 249.

5. Christopher Berry, *The Idea of Luxury: A Conceptual and Historical Investigation* (Cambridge, 1994), see especially chap. 5.

6. R. Galliani, "L'idéologie de la noblesse dans le debat sur le luxe (1699–1756)," in *Études sur le XVIIIe siècle*, vol. 11, *Idéologies de la noblesse*, ed. Roland Mortier and Hervé Hasquin (Brussels, 1984), 53–64.

7. Berry, chap. 5.

8. Linda Levy Peck, *Consuming Splendor: Society and Culture in Seventeenth-Century England* (Cambridge, 2005), 18.

9. Berg and Eger, "Rise and Fall of the Luxury Debates," 8–9.

10. Douglas and Isherwood, 85.

11. Jonathan Brown, *Kings and Connoisseurs: Collecting Art in Seventeenth-Century Europe* (Princeton, 1995), chap. 6.

12. Antoine Schnapper, "The King of France as Collector in the Seventeenth-Century," *Journal of Interdisciplinary History* 17 (1986): 192–202.

13. Marjorie Swann, *Curiosities and Texts: The Culture of Collecting in Early Modern England* (Philadelphia, 2001), 17.

14. Douglas and Isherwood, 118.

15. Schama, *Embarrassment of Riches*, 319.

16. Schama, "Perishable Commodities," 478–88.

17. Chandra Mukerji, "Reading and Writing with Nature: A Materialist Approach to French Formal Gardens," in Brewer and Porter, 439–61.

18. Thornton, *Seventeenth-Century Interior Decoration*, 266.

19. Chandra Mukerji, *Territorial Ambitions and the Gardens of Versailles* (Cambridge, 1997), 176–81.

20. Thornton, *Seventeenth-Century Interior Decoration*, 109, 241–42; Anna Contadini, "Middle Eastern Objects, " in *At Home in Renaissance Italy*, ed. Marta Ajmar-Wollheim and Flora Dennis (London, 2006), 315–18.

21. Thornton, *Seventeenth-Century Interior Decoration*, 241; see also Peter Thornton, *Authentic Décor: The Domestic Interior, 1620–1920* (London, 1984), 59.

22. Thornton, *Seventeenth-Century Interior Decoration*, 108, 132; Henri Havard, *Dictionnaire de l'ameublement et de la decoration depuis le XIIIe siècle jusqu'à nos jours* (Paris, 1890), 1:298.

23. Pardailhé-Galabrun, 147–48.

24. George Leland Hunter, *Tapestries: Their Origin, History, and Renaissance* (New York, 1913), 199–201.

25. Brown, 228–29.

26. Elisa Maillard, *Old French Furniture and Its Surroundings (1610–1815)* (New York, 1925), 3.

27. Sylvie Chadenet, ed., *French Furniture: From Louis XIII to Art Deco* (Boston, 2001), 16–23; Roger de Félice, *French Furniture in the Middle Ages and under Louis XIII* (New York, n.d.), 89–148; Maillard, chap. 1; Esther Singleton, *French and English Furniture: Distinctive Styles and Periods Described and Illustrated* (New York, 1903), 1–34.

28. Chadenet, 24–35; Roger de Félice, *French Furniture under Louis XIV* (London, 1922), 33–109; Maillard, 19–35; Singleton, 65–105. See also Jacques Boulenger, *L'ameublement français au grand siècle* (Paris, 1913).

29. Thornton, *Seventeenth-Century Interior Decoration,* 244–47.

30. Auslander, 78–79.

31. Pardailhé-Galabrun, 74.

32. Pardailhé-Galabrun, 78–80.

33. Thornton, *Seventeenth-Century Interior Decoration,* 149–74.

34. Singleton, 19–20.

35. Thornton, *Seventeenth-Century Interior Decoration,* 168; Singleton, 77, 80. See also Havard, 3:370–94.

36. Singleton, 20–21.

37. Thornton, *Seventeenth-Century Interior Decoration,* 177–79.

38. Clare Vincent, "Magnificent Timekeepers: An Exhibition of Northern European Clocks in New York Collections," *Metropolitan Museum of Art Bulletin,* n.s., 30 (1972): 161.

39. Pardailhé-Galabrun,169.

40. Jules Guiffrey, ed., "Inventaire des meubles précieux de l'Hôtel de Guise en 1644 et en 1688 et de l'Hôtel de Soubise en 1787," *Nouvelles archives de l'art français,* ser. 3, 13 (1896): 156–246.

41. Guiffrey, "Inventaire des meubles précieux de l'Hôtel de Guise."

42. Guiffrey, "Inventaire des meubles précieux de l'Hôtel de Guise."

43. Martin Lister, *A Journey to Paris in the Year 1698,* ed. Raymond Phineas Stearns (Urbana, 1967), 9–10.

44. John Andrews, *A Comparative View of the French and English Nations, in their Manners, Politics, and Literature* (London, 1785). *English Short Title Catalog. Eighteenth Century Collections Online,* 342.

45. Guy Allard, *Historie généalogique des familles* (Grenoble, 1680), 3:87–91.

46. Joseph de Mérindol, Inventaire, 13 B 455, 1680–81, Grenoble—Archives Départementales, Isère (hereafter cited as AD, Isère).

47. Mérindol, Inventaire.

48. Anatole de Gallier, "La Vie de province au XVIIIe siècle d'après les papiers de Franquières et autres documents inédits," *Bulletin de la Société Départementale d'Archéologie et Statistique de la Drome* 9 (1875): 359. See also Hickey, 204.

49. Virieux, 120–21.

50. Gabriel Aymon de Franquières, Inventaire, 13 B 504, 1717–18, AD, Isère.

51. Vincent, "Magnificent Timekeepers," 161.

52. Franquières, Inventaire. On the clockmaker, Claude Duchesne, see G. H. Baillie, *Watches and Clockmakers of the World* (London, 1971).

53. Jean de Vincent, Inventaire, 13 B 474, 1691, AD, Isère.

54. Adolphe Rochas, *Biographie de Dauphiné . . .* (Paris, 1860), 2:482.

55. "Parizet (Seyssins, Seyssinet, Saint-Nizier) fragments d'histoire. Discours de réception de M. de Vernisy," *Bulletin de l'Academie delphinale* 13 (1899), 164–66.

56. Havard, 1:589–90.

57. A. Lacroix, *L'Arrondissement de Montélimar: Géographie, Histoire, Statistique* (Valence, 1888), 7:268–69.

58. François-Alexandre de Perissol-Alleman, Inventaire, 13 B 486, 1708, AD, Isère.

59. M. A. Prudhomme, *Inventaire sommaire des Archives de l'Hôpital de Grenoble* (Grenoble, 1892), 222.

60. A. Gariel, *Bibliothèque historique et littéraire de Dauphiné* (Grenoble, 1864), 2:140–41.

61. Prudhomme, 219–22.

62. Pierre Duchon, Inventaire, 13 B 509, 1719, AD, Isère.

63. Antoine Drogat, Inventaire, 13 B 509, 1719, AD, Isère.

64. Gariel, 129–31.

CHAPTER THREE

1. Mimi Hellman, "The Joy of Sets: The Uses of Seriality in the French Interior," in *Furnishing the Eighteenth Centuruy: What Furniture Can Tell Us about the European and American Past*, ed. Dena Goodman and Kathryn Norberg (New York, 2007), 129.

2. Thornton, *Seventeenth-Century Interior Decoration*, 7–10; Thornton, *Authentic Décor*, 14–15.

3. Alain Mérot, *Retraites mondaines: Aspects de la décoration intérieure à Paris, au XVIIe siècle* (Paris, 1990), 60–61.

4. Mérot, 62–63.

5. Sarah Lowengard, *Color Practices, Color Theories, and the Creation of Color in Objects: Britain and France in the Eighteenth Century* (Ann Arbor: University Microfilms, 1999), 148–49; Havard.

6. Pierre Pizon, Inventaire, 13 B 499, AD, Isère.

7. Lowengard, *Color Practices, Color Theories, and the Creation of Color in Objects*, 148–49.

8. Sarah Lowengard, *The Creation of Color in the Eighteenth-Century Europe* (http://www.gutenberg-e.org/lowengard/index.html), 2–3.

9. Havard, 1:200.

10. Pardailhé-Galabrun, 170–1; Figeac, 48, 292.

11. Pardailhé-Galabrun, 170–71.

12. Sarah Lowengard, "Colours and Colour Making in the Eighteenth Century," in Berg and Clifford, 109.

13. Lowengard, *Color Practices, Color Theories, and the Creation of Color in Objects,* 74.

14. Hellman, "Joy of Sets," 139.

15. Hellman, "Joy of Sets," 131.

16. Thornton, *Seventeenth-Century Interior Decoration,* 97.

17. Thornton, *Seventeenth-Century Interior Decoration,* 130–43; Thornton, "Upholstered Seat Furniture in Europe, 17th and 18th Centuries," in *Upholstery in America and Europe from*

the Seventeenth Century to World War I, ed. Edward S. Cooke Jr. (New York, 1987), 29–38; Margaret Swain, "The Turkey-work Chairs of Holyroodhouse," in Cooke, 51.

18. Thornton, *Authentic Décor,* 59.

19. Thornton, *Authentic Décor,* 9.

20. Hellman, "Joy of Sets," 132.

21. Mimi Hellman, "The Hôtel de Soubise and the Rohan-Soubise Family: Architecture, Interior Decoration, and the Art of Ambition in Eighteenth-Century France" (diss., Princeton, 2000), 2:326.

22. Hellman, "Joy of Sets," 133–34.

23. Thornton, *Authentic Décor,* 60.

24. Havard, 2:966.

25. Franquières, Inventaire.

26. Duchon, Inventaire.

27. Thornton, *Seventeenth-Century Interior Decoration,* 279–80.

28. M. Lainé, *Archives généalogiques et historiques de la noblesse de France* (Paris, 1841), 7:27–29.

29. Anne de la Croix, Inventaire, 13 B 445, 1668, AD, Isère.

30. Perissol-Alleman, Inventaire.

31. Virieux, 243.

32. Pierre de Ponnat, Inventaire, 13 B 480, 1698, AD, Isère.

33. Vincent, Inventaire.

34. Vincent, Inventaire.

35. Franquières, Inventaire.

36. Virieux, 160–61.

37. Abel de Charency, Inventaire, 13 B 498, 1714, AD, Isère.

38. Hickey, 198, 207.

39. Jean Baptiste Rigo, Inventaire, 13 B 493, 1712, AD, Isère.

40. Drogat, Inventaire.

41. Jean Amat, Inventaire, 13 B 485, 1707, AD, Isère.

42. *Dictionnaire des familles françaises anciennes et notables à la fin du XIX siècle* (Evreux, 1903), 1:162.

43. Havard, 2:1090.

44. François Besset, Inventaire, 13 B 498, 1714, AD, Isère.

45. Hellman, "Joy of Sets," 130–31.

46. Hellman, "Joy of Sets," 144–45.

47. Hellman, "Joy of Sets," 147–48.

48. Hellman, "Joy of Sets, 149.

CHAPTER FOUR

1. Clive Edwards, "Reclining Chairs Surveyed: Health, Comfort, and Fashion in Evolving Markets," *Studies in the Decorative Arts,* 6, no. 1 (Fall–Winter 1998–99), 34.

2. John Crowley, *The Invention of Comfort: Sensibilities and Design in Early Modern Britain and Early America* (Baltimore, 2001), 3–6.

3. Joan DeJean, *The Age of Comfort: When Paris Discovered Casual and the Modern Home Began* (New York, 2009).

4. Daniel Roche, *History of Everyday Things,* 107–8; John Crowley, "From Luxury to Comfort and Back Again: Landscape Architecture and the Cottage in Britain and America," in Berg and Eger, *Luxury in the Eighteenth Century,* 135; Pardailhé-Galabrun, 117.

5. Randle Cotgrave, *A Dictionarie of the French and English Tongues* (London, 1611); *Dictionnaire de L'Académie française* (Paris, 1694). See also DeJean, *Age of Comfort,* 6–7.

6. Jules Guiffrey, ed., *Inventaire général du mobilier de la couronne sous Louis XIV* (Paris: 1886), vol. 2; Thornton, *Seventeenth-Century Interior Decoration,* 195–96.

7. Crowley, "From Luxury to Comfort,"146.

8. Thornton, *Seventeenth-Century Interior Decoration,* 195–98, 373, 45; Havard, 1:648, 899.

9. Havard, 1:898–99.

10. Pardailhé-Galabrun, 102; Thornton, *Seventeenth-Century Interior Decoration,* 210–12; Havard, 3:427–32.

11. Thornton, *Seventeenth-Century Interior Decoration,* 210–17.

12. Thornton, *Seventeenth-Century Interior Decoration,* 225.

13. Monique Eleb-Vidal with Anne Debarre-Blanchard, *Architectures de la vie privée, XVIIe–XIXe siècles* (Brussels, 1989), 39, 45–49. See also Pardailhé-Galabrun, 63–66; Scott, 104–5.

14. Scott, 104–5.

15. Thornton, *Seventeenth-Century Interior Decoration,* 296.

16. Mérindol, Inventaire.

17. Vincent, Inventaire.

18. Franquières, Inventaire.

19. Franquières, Inventaire.

20. Jean Miard, Inventaire, 13 B 485, 1707, AD, Isère.

21. Claude Garcin, Inventaire, 13 B 509, 1719, AD, Isère.

22. Jean-Baptiste Garcin–La Mercière, Inventaire, 13 B 498, 1714, AD, Isère.

23. Benoît Chalvet, Inventaire, 13 B 496, 1713, AD, Isère.

24. Figeac, 44–45.

25. McKendrick, Brewer, and Plumb.

26. Crowley, *Invention of Comfort,* 113–15, 120–22, 130–31.

27. Havard, 2:1108–14; Pardailhé-Galabrun, 128; Thornton, *Seventeenth-Century Interior Decoration,* 278–81.

28. Pardailhé-Galabrun, 164.

29. Pardailhé-Galabrun, 164–65; Crowley, *Invention of Comfort,* 124.

30. Franquières, Inventaire.

31. Vincent, Inventaire.

32. Pierre Gleynat, Inventaire, 13 B 452, 1679, AD, Isère.

33. Maxine Berg, *Luxury and Pleasure in Eighteenth-Century Britain,* 250–51.

34. Crowley, *Invention of Comfort,* 149.

35. Crowley, *Invention of Comfort,* 153.

36. Maxine Berg and Helen Clifford, introduction to Berg and Clifford, 4.

37. Goodman, 74.

38. Maxine Berg, "New Commodities, Luxuries and their Consumers in Eighteenth-Century England," 69.

39. de Vries, "Luxury in the Dutch Golden Age in Theory and Practice," 43–44, 51.

40. Paul Langford, *Englishness Identified: Manners and Character, 1650–1850* (Oxford: 2000), 117–19.

41. Andrews.

42. Thornton, *Authentic Décor,* 49.

43. Mimi Hellman, "Furniture, Sociability, and the Work of Leisure in Eighteenth-Century France," *Eighteenth-Century Studies* (1999), 420.

44. Quoted in Hellman, "Furniture," 420.

45. Thornton, *Seventeenth-Century Interior Decoration,* 8–10.

46. Dewald, *Aristocratic Experience,* 15.

47. Dewald, *Aristocratic Experience,* 20–21.

48. Hellman, "Furniture,"437.

49. Langford, 107.

CHAPTER FIVE

1. Barbara Ketcham Wheaton, *Savoring the Past: The French Kitchen and Table from 1300 to 1789* (1983; New York, 1996), 15–16; Roy Strong, *Feast: A History of Grand Eating* (London, 2002), 80.

2. Wheaton, 14–15; Stephen Mennell, *All Manners of Food: Eating and Taste in England and France from the Middle Ages to the Present* (Oxford, 1985), 51.

3. Wheaton, chap. 2.

4. Mennell, 69–71; Wheaton, 34–37.

5. Wheaton, chap. 3.

6. Susan Pinkard, *A Revolution in Taste: The Rise of French Cuisine* (Cambridge, 2009), 30.

7. Wheaton, 114–21.

8. Mennell, 72–73. For more about the cookbooks of the seventeenth and eighteenth centuries, see Philip Hyman and Mary Hyman, "Printing the Kitchen: French Cookbooks, 1480–1800," in *Food: A Culinary History from Antiquity to the Present,* ed. Jean-Louis Flandrin and Massimo Montanari (New York, 1999), chap. 30.

9. T. Sarah Peterson, *Acquired Taste: The French Origins of Modern Cooking* (Ithaca, 1994), chap. 11.

10. Pinkard, 61–64.

11. Pinkard, 73–78.

12. Wheaton, 22–26.

13. Sean Takats, *Corrupting Cooks: Domestic Service and Expertise in Eighteenth-Century France* (Ann Arbor: University Microfilms, 2006), 64–65.

14. L.S.R., *L'Art de bien traiter,* in *L'Art de la cuisine française au XVIIe siècle,* ed. Gilles and Laurence Laurendon (1674; reprint, Paris, 1995), 53–56. For eighteenth-century English translations of the French *batterie de cuisine,* see Isaac Cousteil, *A French idiomatical and critical vocubulary, alphabetically digested . . . Collected from the best French authors, . . . and render'd according to the idioms of both languages . . .* (London, 1748), *English Short Title Catalogue. Eighteenth Century Collections Online.* Also see Abel Boyer, *The complete French master for ladies and gentlemen . . .* (London, 1788). *English Short Title Catalogue. Eighteenth Century Collections OnLine.* For period translations of objects listed in the *batterie de cuisine,* see also "Dictionnaires d'autrefois," *The Artfl Project,* University of Chicago, online, portail.atilf.fr/dictionnaires/onelook.htm. To assist in identifying domestic objects, see Raymond Lecoq, *Les objets de la vie domestique: Utensils en fer de la cuisine et du foyer des origines au XIXe siècle* (Paris, 1979).

15. La Varenne, *Le cuisinier françois: Textes présentées par Jean-Louis Flandrin, Philip Hyman, and Mary Hyman* (Paris, 1983).

16. I am reminded of the woman in the restaurant supply store that I visited in Grenoble. I asked her if one could afford to buy only a single copper pot or pan, which one would it be? She responded without hesitation and handed me a *casserole* of medium size and said it would be this one "for sauces."

17. Pardailhé-Galabrun, 83–87.

18. Franquières, Inventaire.

19. Figeac, 293.

20. Jennifer Davis, *Men of Taste: Gender and Authority in the French Culinary Trades, 1730–1830* (Ann Arbor: University Microfilms, 2004), 179–80.

21. Alain Girard, "Le triomphe de 'La cuisinière bourgeoise,' Livres culinaires, cuisine et société en France aux XVIIe et XVIIIe siècles," *Revue d'histoire moderne et contemporaine* (1977): 497–523.

22. Ponnat, Inventaire.

23. Vincent, Inventaire.

24. Takats, 78–79.

25. Priscilla Parkhurst Ferguson, *Accounting for Taste: The Triumph of French Cuisine* (Chicago, 2004), 36, 43.

26. Ferguson, 44.

27. Pinkard, 79.

28. Pinkard, 78–83.

29. Sara Paston-Williams, *The Art of Dining: A History of Cooking and Eating* (London, 1993), 143–44, 163–64.

30. *Kickshaws* is an English vulgarization, probably intentional, of the French *quelque chose.*

31. Englishman, *The groans of Great-Britain. With a table of the contents. Inscribed to all true Britons by an Englishman* (London, 1753), based on information from *English Short Title Catalogue. Eighteenth Century Collections Online,* 138–39.

32. Joseph Addison, *The Tatler. By the Right Honourable Joseph Addison,* vol. 1 (London, 1777), based on information from *English Short Title Catalogue. Eighteenth Century Collections Online,* no. 148, pp. 189–90.

33. Ken Albala, *The Banquet: Dining in the Great Courts of Late Renaissance Europe* (Urbana, 2007), 121–22.

34. Flandrin, "Distinction through Taste," 3:300–303.

35. Flandrin, "Distinction through Taste," 3:307.

36. Albala, 2–3, 8–9.

37. Takats, 156–60.

38. Takats, 160–64.

39. Flandrin, "Distinction through Taste," 3:300–303.

40. Felicity Heal, "The Idea of Hospitality in Early Modern England," *Past and Present* 102 (1984). See also her much larger work on this subject, *Hospitality in Early Modern England* (Oxford, 1990).

41. Georges Duby, "The Aristocratic Household of Feudal France: Communal Living," in *A History of Private Life,* Vol. 2, *Revelations of the Medieval World,* ed. Georges Duby (Cambridge, MA, 1988), 66–68.

42. Cynthia Kierner, "Hospitality, Sociability, and Gender in the Southern Colonies," *Journal of Southern History* 62 (1996), 451. Writing about the colonial South, Kierner argues that hospitality "strengthened ties of patronage and dependence between superiors and presumed inferiors."

43. Pinkard, 85–87.

44. Antoine Lilti, *Le monde des salons: Sociabilité et mondanité à Paris au XVIIIe siècle* (Paris, 2005), 225–31.

45. Lilti, 225–31.

46. Strong, 231.

47. Ann Eatwell, "A la française to à la russe," in *Elegant Eating: Four Hundred Years of Dining in Style,* ed. Philippa Glanville and Hilary Young (London, 2002), 48.

48. Wheaton, 139.

49. Vincent La Chapelle, *The modern cook: containing instructions for preparing and ordering publick entertainments for the tables of princes* (London, 1736), 1:363. *English Short Title Catalogue. Eighteenth Century Collections Online.*

50. François Massialot, *The Court and Country Cook . . . Faithfully translated out of French into English by J.K.* (London, 1702), in *English Short Title Catalog. Eighteenth-Century Collections on Line.*

51. Flandrin, "Distinction through Taste," 265–70.

52. Helen Clifford, "Knives, Forks, and Spoons, 1600–1830," in Glanville and Young, 54.

53. Pardailhé-Galabrun, 99.

54. Strong, 235. See also Georges Mondgrédien, *La vie quotiedienne sous Louis XIV* (Paris, 1948), 95.

55. Antoine de Courtin, *Nouveau traité de la civilité qui se pratique en France, parmi les honnêtes gens* (1671; ed. Marie-Claire Grassi, 1998), 131. For an early English translation, see *The Rules of civility; or, the maxims of genteel behavior . . . Newly done out of the twelfth edition in French* (London, 1703). *English Short Title Catalog. Eighteenth Century Collections Online.*

56. Courtin, 98.

57. David Mitchell, "Napery, 1600–1800," in Glanville and Young, 52.

58. La Varenne, *Le confiturier françois*, in *Textes présentées par Jean-Louis Flandrin, Philip Hyman, and Mary Hyman* (Paris, 1983), 511–19.

59. Louise Conway Belden, *The Festive Tradition: Table Decoration and Desserts in America, 1650–1900* (New York, 1983), 7–10.

60. Strong, 237–38.

61. Philippa Glanville, "'Saucers,' Casters and Tureens, 1600–1800," in Glanville and Young, 60.

62. Matthew Cock, "The Arrival of the Dinner Service," in *Silver: History and Design*, ed. Philippa Glanville (London, 1996), 40.

63. Thornton, *Seventeenth-Century Interior Decoration*, 286.

64. Ponnat, Inventaire.

65. Thornton, *Seventeenth-Century Interior Decoration*, 282–84.

CONCLUSION

1. Veblen, *Theory of the Leisure Class.* For a succinct discussion of the shortcomings of the Veblen thesis, see Vickery, 274–78.

2. Among these historians are Roger Mettam, *Power and Faction in Louix XIV's France* (London, 1988); William Beik, *Absolutism and Society in Seventeenth-Century France: State Power and Provincial Aristocracy in Languedoc* (Cambridge, 1985); and James B. Collins, *Classes, Estates, and Order in Early Modern Brittany* (Cambridge, 1994).

3. Auslander, 29. My fundamental difference with Auslander's interpretation of the role of Louis XIV has to do with the very real limits to the power of the state and the powerful market force that fashion had come to be.

4. Goodman, 77.

5. Jennifer Jones, "Repackaging Rousseau: Femininity and Fashion in Old Regime France," *French Historical Studies* 18 (Fall 1994), 947; Goodman, 77.

6. Anthony D. Smith, *National Identity* (Reno, 1991), 84–86.

7. Vickery, 278.

8. T. H. Breen, "'Baubles of Britain.'"

9. Breen, "'Baubles of Britain,'" 76.

BIBLIOGRAPHY

ARCHIVAL SOURCES

Grenoble—Archives Départementales, Isère

13 B 445, 1668, Anne de la Croix

13 B 446, 1675, Abel de Buffevant, Gaspard du Beuf

13 B 452, 1679, Pierre Gleynat

13 B 453, 1679, Hugues Bezançon

13 B 455, 1680–81, Joseph de Mérindol

13 B 457, 1681, Anthoinette d'Angilbert; François de Françon; François de la Simiane de la Coste

13 B 463, 1685, Jeanne Richard; Pierre Clément

13 B 466, 1687, Jacques de Vernet

13 B 469, 1688, Jacques Rosset

13 B 472, 1691, Guillaume Fradel: Jean Bertrand; Antoine Bertrand

13 B 474, 1691, Jean de Vincent

13 B 477, 1695, Benoît Brun

13 B 478, 1696, Françoise de la Baume; Philippe Emery

13 B 480, 1698, Pierre de Ponnat

13 B 485, 1707–8, Pierre Martinot; Jean Amat; Jean Miard

13 B 486, 1708, François-Alexandre de Perissol-Alleman

13 B 487, 1709, Claude de Joffrey; Guy Allard; Felicien d'Arzac

13 B 490, 1710, Pierre Aymard; Melchior Cholat; Jean Salomon

13 B 492, 1711, Claude Duclot; Etienne Jullien, Jean de la Robinière; Marie Bonnat

13 B 493, 1712, Jean Baptiste Rigo; Claude Doucet; Philippe Roux; Jean Baptiste Le Juge

13 B 496, 1713, Benoît Chalvet; Jean Baptiste de Valette; Joachim d'Auby

13 B 498, 1714, François Besset, Abel de Charency, Jean Baptiste Garcin–La Mercière, Jean Huide

13 B 499, 1715, Antoine Royer, François d'Allégret, Pierre Pizon
13 B 503, 1716, Charles Pétrequin, Justine de Simiane de La Coste
13 B 504, 1717–18, Gabriel Aymon de Franquières
13 B 509, 1719, Antoine Drogat; Pierre Duchon, Claude Garcin

Grenoble—Bibliothèque Municipale

UNPUBLISHED

R7426. Mélanges Guy Allard. Statistique Nobiliaire. Edited by Hyacinthe Gariel.
"Dénombrement des familles anoblis depuis l'an 1587 jusques en 1634 que ceste
province fut cadastré et leur revenu."
"Familles qui on usurpé la noblesse et qui n'ont point eu de certificat de M. Dugué."
R80, t9, f776. Guy Allard. "Rolle des anoblis dans le Dauphiné depuis 1582 et la
valleur de leurs biens."
U474. "Traité de la noblesse de Dauphiné."

PUBLISHED

Anon. *Abregé des escritures fournies de la part de la noblesse de Dauphiné, contre le
Tiers Estat dudit pais.* n.p., 1600.
Anon. *Premières escritures, pour la defence des Nobles du Dauphiné, contre les de-
mandes et injures de tiers Estats dudit pais.* n.p., 1600.
Anon. *Second escritures pour l'estat des nobles du Dauphiné; contenant contredicts con-
tre la production, et responses aux invectives injurieuses de tiers estat.* Grenoble, 1602.
Anon. *Très humbles remonstrances faites au roy par les Deputez de la Noblesse du
Dauphiné, pour la deffence de leurs droicts et franchises.* Paris, 1633.
Audeyer, Jean-Claude. *Très-humbles remonstrances en forme d'avertissement au roy
par les officiers de la cour de parlement de Dauphiné sur le procès intenté par le tiers
estat.* Grenoble, 1601.
Prudhomme, M. A. *Inventaire sommaire des Archives de l'Hôpital de Grenoble,*
Grenoble, 1892.
Rambaud, Antoine. *Plaidoyé pour le tiers estat de Dauphiné.* Lyon, 1598.
Vincent, Jean. *Discours en forme de plaidoyé pour le tiers estat de Dauphiné.* Paris, 1598.

OTHER PRIMARY SOURCES

Addison, Joseph. *The Tatler. By the Right Honourable Joseph Addison, Esq.* 2 vols.
London, 1777. *English Short Title Catalogue. Eighteenth Century Collections Online.* Gale Group. galenet.galegroup.com/servlet/ECCO.

Allard, Guy. *Dictionnaire historique, chronologique, géographique, généalogique, héraldique, juridique, politique et botanographique de Dauphiné.* 3 vols. Grenoble, 1864.

Allard, Guy. *Historie généalogique des familles.* Vol. 3. Grenoble, 1680. gallica.bnf.fr/ark:/12148/bpt6k840179.

Andrews, John. *A Comparative View of the French and English Nations, in their Manners, Politics, and Literature.* London, 1785. *English Short Title Catalogue. Eighteenth Century Collections Online.* Gale Group. galenet.galegroup.com/servlet/ECCO.

Bellegarde, Jean-Baptiste de Morvan. *The Modes: Or, a Conversation upon the Fashions of all Nations.* London, 1735. English translation.

Boyer, Abel. *The complete French master for ladies and gentlemen. . . .* London, 1788. *English Short Title Catalogue. Eighteenth Century Collections Online.* Gale Group. galenet.galegroup.com/servlet/ECCO.

Chorier, Nicolas. *Histoire générale de Dauphiné.* Grenoble, 1661. Reprint, Valence, 1878.

Cotgrave, Randle. *A Dictionarie of the French and English Tongues.* London, 1611.

Courtin, Antoine de. *Nouveau traité de la civilité qui se pratique en France, parmi les honnêtes gens.* 1671. Edited by Marie-Claire Grassi, Paris, 1998. For an early English translation, see *The Rules of civility; or, the maxims of genteel behavior . . . Newly done out of the twelfth edition in French.* London, 1703. *English Short Title Catalogue. Eighteenth Century Collections Online.* Gale Group. galenet.galegroup.com/servlet/ECCO.

Cousteil, Isaac. *A French idiomatical and critical vocabulary, alphabetically digested . . . Collected from the best French authors, . . . and render'd according to the idioms of both languages. . . .* London, 1748. *English Short Title Catalogue. Eighteenth Century Collections Online.* Gale Group. galenet.galegroup.com/servlet/ECCO.

Dictionnaire de L'Académie française. Paris, 1694.

Dictionnaires d'autrefois. The Artfl Project. artfl-project.uchicago.edu.

Donneau de Visé, Jean. *Mercure galant, 1672–1674.* Geneva, 1982.

Englishman. *The groans of Great-Britain. With a table of the contents. Inscribed to all true Britons by an Englishman.* London, 1753. *English Short Title Catalogue. Eighteenth Century Collections Online.* Gale Group. galenet.galegroup.com/servlet/ECCO.

Guiffrey, Jules, ed. "Inventaire des meubles précieux de l'Hôtel de Guise en 1644 et en 1688 et de l'Hôtel de Soubise en 1787." *Nouvelles archives de l'art français,* ser. 3, 13 (1896): 156–246.

Guiffrey, Jules, ed. *Inventaire général du mobilier de la couronne sous Louis XIV.* 2 vols. Paris, 1886.

La Chapelle, Vincent. *The modern cook: containing instructions for preparing and ordering publick entertainments for the tables of princes.* London, 1736. 3 vols. *English Short Title Catalogue. Eighteenth Century Collections Online.* Gale Group. galenet.galegroup.com/servlet/ECCO.

La Varenne, *Le confiturier françois.* In *Textes présentées par Jean-Louis Flandrin, Philip Hyman, and Mary Hyman.* Paris, 1983.

La Varenne, *Le cuisinier françois: Textes présentées par Jean-Louis Flandrin, Philip Hyman, and Mary Hyman.* Paris, 1983.

Lister, Martin. *A Journey to Paris in the Year 1698.* Edited by Raymond Phineas Stearns. Urbana, 1967.

L.S.R. *L'Art de bien traiter.* In *L'Art de la cuisine française au XVIIe siècle.* Edited by Gilles and Laurence Laurendon. 1694. Reprint, Paris, 1995.

Massialot, François. *Le Nouveau cuisinier royal et bourgeois ou cuisinier moderne,* Vol. 2. Paris, 2005. For an early English translation, see *The Court and Country Cook ... Faithfully translated out of French into English by J.K.* London, 1702. *English Short Title Catalog. Eighteenth-Century Collections on Line.* Gale Group. galenet.gale group.com/servlet/ECCO.

Saint-Evremond. *Oeuvres de Monsieur de Saint-Evremond, publiées sur les manuscrits de l'auteur.* 6 vols. London, 1725. *English Short Title Catalogue. Eighteenth Century Collections Online.* Gale Group. galenet.galegroup.com/servlet/ECCO. For an early English translation, see *The works of Monsieur de St. Evremond, made English from the French original: with the Life of the author; by Mr. des Maizeaux, ... To which are added the memoirs of the Dutchess of Mazarin, &c.* 3 vols. 2nd ed., corrected and enlarged. London, 1728. *English Short Title Catalogue. Eighteenth Century Collections Online.* Gale Group. galenet.galegroup.com/servlet/ECCO.

Virieux, Maurice. "Le Parlement de Grenoble au XVIIe siècle: Étude sociale." Thèse de doctorat d'état, Paris, 1986.

SECONDARY SOURCES

Albala, Ken. *The Banquet: Dining in the Great Courts of Late Renaissance Europe.* Urbana, 2007.

Anderson, Benedict. *Imagined Communities: Reflections on the Origins and Spread of Nationalism.* London, 1983.

Arminjon, Catherine. "L'utile et l'agréable: Le décor de la table du XVe au XIXe siècle." In *La Table et le partage,* 67–78. Paris, 1986.

Auslander, Leora. *Taste and Power: Furnishing Modern France.* Berkeley, 1996.

Baillie, G. H. *Watches and Clockmakers of the World.* London, 1971.

Baudrillart, H. *Histoire de luxe privé et public depuis l'antiquité jusqu'à nos jours.* 4 vols. Paris, 1881.

Beik, William. *Absolutism and Society in Seventeenth-Century France: State and Provincial Aristocracy in Languedoc.* Cambridge, 1985.

Belden, Louise Conway. *The Festive Tradition: Table Decoration and Desserts in America, 1650–1900.* New York, 1983.

Bell, David. "Recent Works on Early Modern French National Identity." *Journal of Modern History* 68 (1996): 84–113.

Belmont, Alain. "L'Intégration au royaume par les armes: Le Dauphiné et les guerres en Italie." In *Dauphiné, France: De la principauté indépendante à la province (XIIe–XVIIIe siècles),* edited by Vital Chomel, 109–22. Grenoble, 1999.

Benhamou, Reed. "Fashion in the *Mercure:* From Human Foible to Female Failing." *Eighteenth-Century Studies* 31 (1997): 27–43.

Berg, Maxine. *Luxury and Pleasure in Eighteenth-Century Britain.* Oxford, 2005.

Berg, Maxine. "New Commodities, Luxuries, and Their Consumers in Eighteenth-Century England." *Consumers and Luxury: Consumer Culture in Europe, 1650–1850,* edited by Maxine Berg and Helen Clifford, 63–87. Manchester, 1999.

Berg, Maxine, and Helen Clifford, eds. *Consumers and Luxury: Consumer Culture in Europe, 1650–1850.* Manchester, 1999.

Berg, Maxine, and Elizabeth Eger. "The Rise and Fall of the Luxury Debates." In *Luxury in the Eighteenth Century: Debates, Desires and Delectable Goods,* edited by Maxine Berg and Elizabeth Eger, 7–27. London, 2003.

Berry, Christopher. *The Idea of Luxury: A Conceptual and Historical Investigation.* Cambridge, 1994.

Bohanan, Donna. "Color Schemes and Decorative Tastes in the Nobles Houses of Old Regime Dauphiné." In *Furnishing the Eighteenth Century: What Furniture Can Tell Us about the European and American Past,* edited by Dena Goodman and Kathryn Norberg, 117–28. New York, 2007.

Bohanan, Donna. *Crown and Nobility in Early Modern France.* London, 2001.

Bondel, Nicole. "L'utilité des objets de la table." In *La Table et le partage,* 79–88. Paris, 1986.

Bonnet, Jean-Claude. "La Naissance de la gastronomie et l'écriture gourmande." In *Consuming Culture: The Arts of the French Table,* edited by John West-Sooby, 2–10. Cranbury, NJ, 2004.

Boulenger, Jacques. *L'ameublement français au grand siècle.* Paris, 1913.

Bourdieu, Pierre. *Distinction: A Social Critique of the Judgement of Taste.* Cambridge, MA, 1984.

Breen, T. H. "'Baubles of Britain': The American and Consumer Revolutions of the Eighteenth Century." *Past and Present* 119 (May 1988): 73–104.

Breen, T. H. "The Empire of Goods: The Anglicization of Colonial America, 1690–1776." *Journal of British Studies* 25 (1986): 467–99.

Brewer, John, and Roy Porter, eds. *Consumption and the World of Goods.* London, 1993.

Brown, Jonathan . *Kings and Connoisseurs: Collecting Art in Seventeenth-Century Europe.* Princeton, 1995.

Burke, Peter. "Conspicuous Consumption in Seventeenth-Century Italy." In *The Historical Anthropology of Early Modern Italy,* edited by Peter Burke, 132–49. Cambridge, 1987.

Campbell, Colin. *The Romantic Ethic and the Spirit of Modern Consumerism.* London, 1987.

Campbell, Colin. "Understanding Traditional and Modern Patterns of Consumption in Eighteenth-Century England: A Character-Action Approach." *Consumption and the World of Goods,* edited by John Brewer and Roy Porter, 40–57. London, 1993.

Chadenet, Sylvie, ed. *French Furniture: From Louis XIII to Art Deco.* Boston, 2001.

Chartier, Roger, ed. *A History of Private Life.* Vol. 3, *Passions of the Renaissance.* Cambridge, MA, 1989.

Chomel, Vital. "La monarchie, 'Etat de justice,' et le conflit des ordres en Dauphiné: Autour du procès des tailles, 1540–1640." *Cahiers d'histoire* 33 (1988): 71–81.

Clifford, Helen. "Knives, Forks, and Spoons, 1600–1830." In *Elegant Eating: Four Hundred Years of Dining in Style,* edited by Philippa Glanville and Hilary Young, 54–57. London, 2002.

Cock, Matthew. "The Arrival of the Dinner Service." In *Silver: History and Design,* edited by Philippa Glanville, 38–41. London, 1996.

Collins, James B. *Classes, Estates, and Order in Early Modern Brittany.* Cambridge, 1994.

Constant, Jean-Marie. *La noblesse française aux XVIe–XVIIe siècles.* Paris, 1985.

Contadini, Anna. "Middle Eastern Objects." In *At Home in Renaissance Italy,* edited by Marta Ajmar-Wollheim and Flora Dennis, 308–21. London, 2006.

Cooke, Edward S., Jr., ed. *Upholstery in America and Europe: From the Seventeenth Century to World War I.* New York, 1987.

Coquery, Natasha. *L'espace du pouvoir: De la demeure privée à l'édifice public, Paris, 1700–1790.* Paris, 2000.

Coquery, Natasha. *L'Hôtel aristocratique: Le marché du luxe à Paris au XVIIIe siècle.* Paris, 1998.

Coulomb, Clarisse. "Héritages familiaux, solidarités professionnelles et théâtre politique: L'habitat parlementaire à Grenoble dans le seconde moitié du XVIIIe siècle." *Histoire urbaine* 1 (2002): 5–25.

Crouzet, François. "England and France in the Eighteenth-Century: A Comparative Analysis of Two Economic Growths." In *The Causes of the Industrial Revolution in England*, edited by R. M. Hartwell, 139–74. London, 1967.

Crowley, John. "From Luxury to Comfort and Back Again: Landscape Architecture and the Cottage in Britain and America." In *Luxury in the Eighteenth Century*, edited by Maxine Berg and Elizabeth Eger, 135–50. London, 2003.

Crowley, John. *The Invention of Comfort: Sensibilities and Design in Early Modern Britain and Early America*. Baltimore, 2001.

Davis, Jennifer. *Men of Taste: Gender and Authority in the French Culinary Trades, 1730–1830*. Ann Arbor: University Microfilms, 2004.

DeJean, Joan. *The Age of Comfort: When Paris Discovered Casual and the Modern Home Began*. New York, 2009.

DeJean, Joan. *Ancients against Moderns: Culture Wars and the Making of a Fin de Siècle*. Chicago, 1997.

DeJean, Joan. *The Essence of Style: How the French Invented High Fashion, Fine Food, Chic Cafés, Style, Sophistication, and Glamour*. New York, 2005.

de Vries, Jan. "Luxury in the Dutch Golden Age in Theory and Practice." In *Luxury in the Eighteenth Century: Debates, Desires and Delectable Goods*, edited by Maxine Berg and Elizabeth Eger, 41–56. London, 2003.

Dewald, Jonathan. *Aristocratic Experience and the Origins of Modern Culture: France, 1570–1715*. Berkeley, 1993.

Dewald, Jonathan. *The European Nobility, 1400–1600*. Cambridge, 1996.

Dictionnaire des familles françaises anciennes et notables à la fin du XIX siècle. Vol. 1. Evreux, 1903.

Douglas, Mary, and Baron Isherwood. *The World of Goods: Towards an Anthropology of Consumption*. New York, 1979.

Drouard, Alain. *Les Français et la table: Alimentation, cuisine, gastronomie du Moyen Âge à nos jours*. Paris, 2005.

Duby, Georges. "The Aristocratic Household of Feudal France: Communal Living." *A History of Private Life*. Vol. 2, *Revelations of th Medieval World*, edited by Georges Duby, 35–155. Cambridge, MA, 1988.

Eatwell, Ann. "A la française to à la russe." In *Elegant Eating: Four Hundred Years of Dining in Style*, edited by Philippa Glanville and Hilary Young, 48–51. London, 2002.

Edwards, Clive. *Eighteenth-Century Furniture*. Manchester, 1996.

Edwards, Clive. "Reclining Chairs Surveyed: Health, Comfort, and Fashion in Evolving Markets." *Studies in the Decorative Arts* 6, no. 1 (Fall–Winter 1998–99): 32–67.

Edwards, Clive. *Turning Houses into Homes: A History of the Retailing and Consumption of Domestic Furnishings*. Aldershot, 2005.

Eleb-Vidal, Monique, with Anne Debarre-Blanchard. *Architectures de la vie privée, XVIIe–XIXe siècles*. Brussels, 1989.

Elias, Norbert. *The Court Society*. New York, 1983.

Fairchilds, Cissie. "The Production and Marketing of Populuxe Goods in Eighteenth-Century Paris." In *Consumption and the World of Goods*, edited by John Brewer and Roy Porter, 228–48. London, 1993.

Favier, René. "De la principauté à la province: La perte des libertés dauphinoises (XVIe–XVIIe siècle)." In *Dauphiné, France: De la principauté indépendante à la province (XIIe–XVIIIe siècles)*, edited by Vital Chomel, 123–45. Grenoble, 1999.

Félice, Roger de. *French Furniture in the Middle Ages and under Louis XIII*. New York, n.d.

Félice, Roger de. *French Furniture under Louis XIV*. London, 1922.

Ferguson, Priscilla Parkhurst. *Accounting for Taste: The Triumph of French Cuisine*. Chicago, 2004.

Figeac, Michel. *La douceur des Lumières: Noblesse et art de vivre en Guyenne au XVIIIe siècle*. Paris, 2001.

Flandrin, Jean-Louis. *Arranging the Meal: A History of Table Service in France*. Berkley, 2007.

Flandrin, Jean-Louis. "Distinction through Taste." In *A History of Private Life*. Vol. 3, *Passions of the Renaissance*, edited by Roger Chartier, 265–307. Cambridge, MA, 1989.

Fox, Robert, and Anthony Turner. *Luxury Trades and Consumerism in Ancien Régime Paris*. Aldershot, 1998.

Galliani, R. "L'idéologie de la noblesse dans le debat sur le luxe (1699–1756)." In *Études sur le XVIIIe siècle*. Vol. 11, *Idéologies de la noblesse*, edited by Roland Mortier and Hervé Hasquin, 53–64. Brussels, 1984.

Gallier, Anatole de. "La Vie de province au XVIIIe siècle d'après les papiers de Franquières et autres documents inédits." *Bulletin de la Société Départementale d'Archéologie et Statistique de la Drome* 9 (1875): 355–77.

Gariel, A. *Bibliothèque historique et littéraire de Dauphiné*. Vol. 2. Grenoble, 1864.

Girard, Alain. "Le triomphe de 'La cuisinière bourgeoise': Livres culinaires, cuisine et société en France aux XVIIe et XVIIIe siècles." *Revue d'histoire moderne et contemporaine* 23 (1977): 497–523.

Girard, Sylvie. *Histoire des objets de cuisine et de gourmandise.* Paris, 1991.

Girouard, Mark. *Life in the French Country House.* New York, 2000.

Glanville, Philippa. "'Saucers,' Casters and Tureens, 1600–1800." In *Elegant Eating: Four Hundred Years of Dining in Style,* edited by Philippa Glanville and Hilary Young, 60–63. London, 2002.

Gloag, John. *Guide to Furniture Styles: English and French, 1450–1850.* New York, 1972.

Godard de Donville, Louise. *Signification de la mode sous Louis XIII.* Aix-en-Provence, 1976.

Goldthwaite, Richard A. *Wealth and the Demand for Art in Italy, 1300–1600.* Baltimore, 1993.

Goodman, Dena. "Furnishing Discourses: Readings of a Writing Desk in Eighteenth-Century France." In *Luxury in the Eighteenth Century: Debates, Desires and Delectable Goods,* edited by Maxine Berg and Elizabeth Eger, 71–88. London, 2003.

Goodman, Dena, and Kathryn Norberg, eds. *Furnishing the Eighteenth Century: What Furniture Can Tell Us about the European and American Past.* New York, 2007.

Gronow, Jukka. *The Sociology of Taste.* London, 1997.

Havard, Henri. *Dictionnaire de l'ameublement et de la décoration depuis le XIIIe siècle jusqu'à nos jours.* 4 vols. Paris, 1890.

Heal, Felicity. *Hospitality in Early Modern England.* Oxford, 1990.

Heal, Felicity. "The Idea of Hospitality in Early Modern England." *Past and Present* 102 (1984): 66–93.

Hellman, Mimi. "Firedogs and the Tensions of the Hearth." In *Taking Shape: Finding Sculpture in the Decorative Arts* (Los Angeles, 2009), 176–85.

Hellman, Mimi. "Furniture, Sociability, and the Work of Leisure in Eighteenth-Century France." *Eighteenth-Century Studies* (1999): 415–45.

Hellman, Mimi. "The Hôtel de Soubise and the Rohan-Soubise Family: Architecture, Interior Decoration, and the Art of Ambition in Eighteenth-Century France." 3 vols. Diss., Princeton, 2000.

Hellman, Mimi. "The Joy of Sets: The Uses of Seriality in the French Interior. " In *Furnishing the Eighteenth Century: What Furniture Can Tell Us about the European and American Past,* edited by Dena Goodman and Kathryn Norberg, 129–53. New York, 2007.

Hickey, Daniel. *The Coming of French Absolutism: The Struggle for Tax Reform in the Province of Dauphiné, 1540–1640.* Toronto, 1986.

Hinckley, F. Lewis. *A Directory of Antique French Furniture, 1735–1800.* New York, 1967.

Hunter, George Leland. *Tapestries: Their Origin, History, and Renaissance.* New York, 1913.

Hyman, Philip, and Mary Hyman. "Printing the Kitchen: French Cookbooks, 1480–1800." In *Food: A Culinary History from Antiquity to the Present,* edited by Jean-Louis Flandrin and Massimo Montanari, 394–402. New York, 1999.

Jones, Colin. *The Great Nation: France from Louis XV to Napoleon.* London, 2003.

Jones, Colin, and Rebecca Spang. "Sans-culottes, Sans Café, Sans Tabac: Shifting Realms of Necessity and Luxury in Eighteenth-Century France." In *Consumers and Luxury: Consumer Culture in Europe, 1650–1850,* edited by Maxine Berg and Helen Clifford, 37–62. Manchester, 1999.

Jones, Jennifer. "Repackaging Rousseau: Femininity and Fashion in Old Regime France." *French Historical Studies* 18 (Fall 1994); 939–67.

Jones, Jennifer. *Sexing* La Mode: *Gender, Fashion and Commercial Culture in Old Regime France.* Oxford, 2004.

Jouanna, Arlette. *Le devoir de révolte: La noblesse française et la gestation de l'état moderne (1559–1661).* Paris, 1989.

Kierner, Cynthia. "Hospitality, Sociability, and Gender in the Southern Colonies." *Journal of Southern History* 62 (1996): 449–80.

Kwass, Michael. "Ordering the World of Goods: Consumer Revolution and the Classification of Objects in Eighteenth-Century France." *Representations* 82 (2003): 87–116.

Lacroix, A. *L'Arrondissement de Montélimar: Géographie, Histoire, Statistique.* Vol. 7. Valence, 1888.

Lainé, M. *Archives généalogiques et historiques de la noblesse de France.* Vol. 7. Paris, 1841.

Langford, Paul. *Englishness Identified: Manners and Character, 1650–1850.* Oxford, 2000.

Lecoq, Raymond. *Les objets de la vie domestique: Utensils en fer de la cuisine et du foyer des origines au XIXe siècle.* Paris, 1979.

Lilti, Antoine. *Le monde des salons: Sociabilité et mondanité à Paris au XVIIIe siècle.* Paris, 2005.

Lowengard, Sarah. "Practices, Color Theories, and the Creation of Color in Objects: Britain and France in the Eighteenth Century." Ann Arbor: University Microfilms, 1999.

Lowengard, Sarah. "Colours and Colour Making in the Eighteenth Century." In *Consumers and Luxury: Consumer Culture in Europe, 1650–1850,* edited by Maxine Berg and Helen Clifford, 109. Manchester, 1999.

Lowengard, Sarah. *The Creation of Color in Eighteenth-Century Europe.* www.gutenberg-e.org/lowengard/index.html.

Magendie, Maurice. *La politesse mondaine et les théories de l'honnêteté, en France, au XVIIe siècle, de 1600 à 1660.* 2 vols. Paris, 1925.

Maillard, Elisa. *Old French Furniture and Its Surroundings (1610–1815)*. New York, 1925.

Major, J. Russell. *Representative Institutions in Early Modern France*. New Haven, 1980.

Martin, Ann Smart. "Material Things and Cultural Meanings: Notes on the Study of Early American Material Culture." In *William and Mary Quarterly* 53 (1996): 5–12.

Maza, Sarah. "Luxury, Morality, and Social Change: Why There Was No Middle-Class Consciousness in Prerevolutionary France." *Journal of Modern History* 69 (1997): 199–229.

McCracken, Grant. *Culture and Consumption.* Bloomington, 1988.

McKendrick, Neil, John Brewer, and J. H. Plumb. *The Birth of a Consumer Society: The Commercialization of Eighteenth-Century England*. Bloomington, 1982.

Mennell, Stephen. *All Manners of Food: Eating and Taste in England and France from the Middle Ages to the Present*. Oxford, 1985.

Mérot, Alain. *Retraites mondaines: Aspects de la décoration intérieure à Paris, au XVIIe siècle*. Paris, 1990.

Mettam, Roger. *Power and Faction in Louis XIV's France*. London, 1988.

Miller, Lesley Ellis. " Paris–Lyon–Paris: Dialogue in the Design and Distribution of Patterned Silks in the 18th Century." In *Luxury Trades and Consumerism in Ancien Régime Paris,* edited by Robert Fox and Anthony Turner, 139–67. Aldershot, 1998.

Mitchell, David. "Napery, 1600–1800." In *Elegant Eating: Four Hundred Years of Dining in Style,* edited by Philippa Glanville and Hilary Young, 52–53. London, 2002.

Mondgrédien, Georges. *La vie quotiedienne sous Louis XIV*. Paris, 1948.

Moriarity, Michael. *Taste and Ideology in Seventeenth-Century France*. Cambridge, 1988.

Motley, Mark. *Becoming a French Aristocrat: The Education of the Court Nobility, 1580–1715*. Princeton, 1990.

Muchembled, Robert. "Luxe et dynamisme social à Douai au 17e siècle." In *Nouvelles approches concernant la culture de l'habitat,* edited by R. Baetens and B. Blondé, 197–211. Turnhout, 1991.

Mukerji, Chandra. "Reading and Writing with Nature: A Materialist Approach to French Formal Gardens." In *Consumption and the World of Goods,* edited by John Brewer and Roy Porter, 439–61. London, 1993.

Mukerji, Chandra. *Territorial Ambitions and the Gardens of Versailles*. Cambridge, 1997.

Nenadic, Stana. "Middle Class Consumers and Domestic Culture in Edinburgh and Glasgow, 1720–1840." *Past and Present* 145 (1994): 122–56.

Neuschel, Kristen B. "Noble Households in the Sixteenth Century: Material Settings and Human Communities." *French Historical Studies* 15 (1988): 599–601.

Neuschel, Kristen B. *Word of Honor: Interpreting Noble Culture in Sixteenth-Century France*. Ithaca, 1989.

Norberg, Kathryn. *Rich and Poor in Grenoble, 1600–1814*. Berkeley, 1985.

Pardailhé-Galabrun, Annik. *The Birth of Intimacy: Privacy and Domestic Life in Early Modern Paris*. London, 1991.

"Parizet (Seyssins, Seyssinet, Saint-Nizier) fragments d'histoire: Discours de réception de M. de Vernisy." *Bulletin de l'Academie delphinale* 13 (1899): 109–335.

Parker, David. *Class and State in Ancien Régime France: The Road to Modernity?* London, 1996.

Paston-Williams, Sara. *The Art of Dining: A History of Cooking and Eating*. London, 1993.

Peck, Linda Levy. *Consuming Splendor: Society and Culture in Seventeenth-Century England*. Cambridge, 2005.

Perrot, Philippe. *Le Luxe: Une richesse entre faste et confort, XVIIIe–XIXe siècle*. Paris, 1995.

Peterson, T. Sarah. *Acquired Taste: The French Origins of Modern Cooking*. Ithaca, 1994.

Pinkard, Susan. *A Revolution in Taste: The Rise of French Cuisine*. Cambridge, 2009.

Ponsonby, Margaret. *Stories from Home: English Domestic Interiors, 1750–1850*. Aldershot, 2007.

Poulain, Jean-Pierre, and Edmond Neirinck. *Histoire de la cuisine et des cuisiniers: Techniques culinaires et pratiques de table en France, du Moyen Âge à nos jours*. Paris, 2004.

Ranum, Orest. "Courtesy, Absolutism, and the Rise of the French State." *Journal of Modern History* 52 (1980): 426–51.

Ranum, Orest. *Paris in the Age of Absolutism: An Essay*. University Park, PA, 2002.

Revel, Jacques. "The Uses of Civility." In *A History of Private Life*. Vol. 3, *Passions of the Renaissance*, edited by Roger Chartier, 167–205. Cambridge, MA, 1989.

Reyniès, Nicole de. *Le mobilier domestique: Vocabulaire typologique*. 2 vols. Paris, 1992.

Rochas, Adolphe. *Biographie de Dauphiné. . . .* 2 vols. Paris, 1860.

Roche, Daniel. *The Culture of Clothing: Dress and Fashion in the Ancien Régime*. Cambridge, 1994.

Roche, Daniel. *A History of Everyday Things: The Birth of Consumption in France, 1600–1800*. Cambridge, 2000.

Roche, Daniel. *The People of Paris: An Essay in Popular Culture in the Eighteenth Century*. Los Angeles, 1987.

Sargentson, Carolyn. *Merchants and Luxury Markets: The Marchands Merciers of Eighteenth-Century Paris*. London, 1996.

Sarti, Raffaella. *Europe at Home: Family and Material Culture, 1500–1800*. New Haven, 2002.

Schalk, Ellery. *From Valor to Pedigree: Ideas of Nobility in France in the Sixteenth and Seventeenth Centuries*. Princeton, 1986.

Schama, Simon. *The Embarassment of Riches: An Interpretation of Dutch Culture in the Golden Age*. New York, 1987.

Schama, Simon. "Perishable Commodities: Dutch Still-Life Painting and the 'Empire of Things.'" In *Consumption and the World of Goods*, edited by John Brewer and Roy Porter, 478–88. London. 1993.

Schnapper, Antoine. "The King of France as Collector in the Seventeenth-Century." *Journal of Interdisciplinary History* 17 (1986): 185–202.

Scott, Katie. *The Rococo Interior: Decoration and Social Spaces in Early Eighteenth-Century Paris*. New Haven, 1995.

Scott, Katie, and Deborah Cherry, eds. *Between Luxury and the Everyday: Decorative Arts in Eighteenth-Century France*. London, 2005.

Sewell, William H., Jr. "The Empire of Fashion and the Rise of Capitalism in Eighteenth-Century France. " *Past and Present* 206 (2010): 81–120.

Shovlin, John. "The Cultural Politics of Luxury in Eighteenth-Century France." *French Historical Studies* 23 (2000): 577–606.

Singleton, Esther. *French and English Furniture: Distinctive Styles and Periods Described and Illustrated*. New York, 1903.

Smith, Anthony D. *National Identity*. Reno, 1991.

Smith, Woodruff D. *Consumption and the Making of Respectability, 1600–1800*. New York, 2002.

Sonenscher, Michael. *Work and Wages. Natural Law, Politics, and the Eighteenth-Century French Trades*. Cambridge, 1989.

Strange, Thomas Arthur. *French Interiors, Furniture, Decoration, Woodwork, and Allied Arts during the Last Half of the Seventeenth Century, the Whole of the Eighteenth Century, and the Early Part of the Nineteenth Century*. New York, 1968.

Strong, Roy. *Feast: A History of Grand Eating*. London, 2002.

Styles, John. "Product Innovation in Early Modern London." *Past and Present* 168 (2000): 124–69.

Styles, John, and Amanda Vickery. Introduction to *Gender, Taste, and Material Culture in Britain and North American, 1700–1830*, edited by John Styles and Amanda Vickery, 1–34. New Haven, 2007.

Swain, Margaret. "The Turkey-work Chairs of Holyroodhouse." In *Upholstery in America and Europe: From the Seventeenth Century to World War I*, edited by Edward S. Cooke Jr., 51–64. New York, 1987.

Swann, Marjorie. *Curiosities and Texts: The Culture of Collecting in Early Modern England.* Philadelphia, 2001.

Takats, Sean. *Corrupting Cooks: Domestic Service and Expertise in Eighteenth-Century France.* Ann Arbor: University Microfilms, 2006.

Thornton, Peter *Authentic Décor: The Domestic Interior, 1620–1920.* London, 1984.

Thornton, Peter. *Seventeenth-Century Interior Decoration in England, France and Holland.* New Haven, 1978.

Thornton, Peter. "Upholstered Seat Furniture in Europe, 17th and 18th Centuries." In *Upholstery in America and Europe from the Seventeenth Century to World War I,* edited by Edward S. Cooke Jr., 29–38. New York, 1987.

Van Doren, Liewain Scott. "Revolt and Reaction in the City of Romans, Dauphiné, 1579–1580." *Sixteenth Century Journal* 5 (1974): 71–100.

Veblen, Thorstein. *The Theory of the Leisure Class: An Economic Study of Institutions.* Fairfield, NJ, 1991.

Verlet, Pierre. *French Furniture of the Eighteenth Century.* Charlottesville, 1991.

Vickery, Amanda. "Women and the World of Goods: A Lancashire Consumer and Her Possessions, 1751–81." In *Consumption and the World of Goods,* edited by John Brewer and Roy Porter, 274–301. London, 1993.

Vincent, Clare. "Magnificent Timekeepers: An Exhibition of Northern European Clocks in New York Collections." *Metropolitan Museum of Art Bulletin,* n.s., 30 (1972): 154–65.

Waquet, Françoise. "La Mode au XVIIe siècle: De la folie à l'usage." *Cahiers de l'AIEF* 38 (1986): 91–124.

Weatherill, Lorna. "The Meaning of Consumer Behavior in Late Seventeenth- and Early Eighteenth-Century England. In *Consumption and the World of Goods,* edited by John Brewer and Roy Porter, 206–27. London, 1993.

Weir, David. "Les crises économiques et les origines de la Révolution française." *Annales: Economies, Sociétés, Civilisations* 46 (1991): 917–47.

West-Sooby, John, ed. *Consuming Culture: The Arts of the French Table.* Cranbury, NJ, 2004.

Wheaton, Barbara Ketcham. *Savoring the Past: The French Kitchen and Table from 1300 to 1789.* 1983. New York, 1996.

Whitehead, John. *The French Interior in the Eighteenth Century.* New York, 1993.

INDEX